PONIES AN

Other titles by Mary Gervaise in Armada

A Pony from the Farm
Ponies and Mysteries
The Vanishing Pony
A Pony of Your Own

First published in the U.K. in 1950 by Lutterworth Press, London. This edition was first published in 1969 by William Collins Sons & Co. Ltd., 14 St. James's Place, London S.W.1.

This edition 1974

Printed in Great Britain by
Love & Malcomson Ltd.,
Brighton Road, Redhill, Surrey.

PONIES AND HOLIDAYS

MARY GERVAISE

CONTENTS

CHAPTER ONE

EXTREMES MEET

GEORGIE KANE had no idea that she was wearing a beaming smile on her face as she walked up and down Platform 5. Had she known, she would have removed it at once, because she was rather shy and disliked attracting attention. There were a good many people waiting at Fontayne Junction on that sunny April afternoon, and she did wonder a little why they were regarding her with such friendly interest. She amused herself by studying them each time she passed, making up stories about where they were going and who would meet them when they got there. But—although she invented wonderful adventures for them all—she wouldn't have changed places with a single one of them.

The down train was late. When she had examined everything on the bookstall, and peered for the third time into the big wicker cage in which several racing pigeons were travelling to Cornwall, she moved to the edge of the platform to gaze up the line. And all the time her smile of anticipation was growing wider and wider.

"You looks happy, love," said a voice in her ear—a queer, cracked voice, like that of an amiable cockatoo. It belonged to an old gipsy woman who was sitting serenely on a heap of knobbly-looking bundles.

Georgie looked round to see who "love" could be, and then saw with some embarrassment that the remark had been addressed to her.

"Yes, I am, thank you," she answered, looking at the brown, leathery face with its countless wrinkles and lines. "I'm waiting for two friends who are coming to stay with me."

"And a nice clack o' tongues there'll be," chuckled the crone, "though ye've not been parted long . . ."

"Well, no, we haven't," Georgie admitted. "Only two weeks. But—how did you know?"

"A maidie like you be too young to have known long partings."

"Oh, I see." Georgie was rather disappointed to

"And I be ninety-four come July."

find that there was no magic here. "But I'm not exactly *young*, you know. I'll be fourteen in August——"

"And I be ninety-four come July," laughed the old gipsy, "and I can't travel the roads no more. But I'm waiting for friends, same as you, love, and they'll take me on to the moors where I'll feel young again. Here comes the train."

Georgie looked up the line again, and shook her head.

"There's no smoke yet, and it isn't even signalled."

But the signal clicked even as she spoke, and the old woman nodded.

"I hear it, love. Old Sarah's ears be as keen as ever. So make ready to greet your friends, and may you still be happy next time I set eyes on ye——"

"Next time——?" Georgie shivered a little. There really *was* something uncanny about those jet-black eyes.

"Aye," said the gipsy, and nodded emphatically. "But there's much to be gone through before then. I see things lost and things found—but there, my old tongue do keep runnin' on. Here's your train, love."

Yes, there was a puff of white smoke on the horizon, and Georgie grew tense with excitement. She was longing to take Susan and Patience home with her, and introduce them to the family, and show them everything. She could scarcely believe that four months ago she hadn't known that they existed.

The big train stopped at the junction, and several people got out. Georgie looked for Susan's red head and Patience's fair one. She saw them at once, for the girls were waving wildly, as they opened the door of the compartment which they had to themselves. Susan dragged Georgie into it, for it had been arranged that she should travel with them to Driscoe, the station nearest her home.

"Sue—Patience—isn't this super?" cried Georgie, as the train began to move, and they all subsided in a heap on the seat. "It's lovely to know that we've got a whole fortnight ahead of us before school starts again. Oh, you remember that Rough and Tough were going away to stay with friends? They're not, now. The friends have got measles. So it will be a bit of a squash, but much more fun really——"

"Oh, goody—I've been wanting to meet the Lads," laughed Susan, using quite naturally the nickname which Georgie's twin brothers had acquired. "I say, it *is* wizard to see you—but I hope it's not much farther to Discoe. I'm starving. I've been gnawing my racquet ever since Exeter——"

"Sue, you're awful," said Patience, with a wan smile. "You know you've had lunch and tea on the train. How—how are you, Georgie? Guardie asked to be remembered to you. . . ."

She was very nervous, Georgie could see. Her pretty face was pale beneath the old-fashioned straw hat she wore, and her hands in their prim cotton gloves were clasped tightly in her blue serge lap. Patience Best, who lived with a very old guardian and his housekeeper, always looked as though she belonged to a bygone age.

This was the first time she had ever set out to visit anyone else's home, and though she had been delighted when Georgie first issued the invitation, she was now wishing most heartily that she had refused it. The knowledge that she was to meet the fourteen-year-old twins was a fresh cause of alarm. She had mixed very little with girls of her own age before she went to the Grange School last term, and about boys she knew nothing at all. From various books she had read, she gathered that they were always playing terrifying practical jokes, or teasing people, or carrying frogs about in their pockets. . . . She tried to look happy and at ease, for Georgie and Susan were obviously agog with happiness. But she wished that the train would turn round and deposit her safely at Lennet Magna, the lovely village on the Dorset-Hampshire border where she had lived ever since she could remember.

"I've come prepared for *everything*," Susan was saying eagerly, as she indicated a huge pile of luggage on the rack. "There's more in the van. I've brought my racquet, of course, and hockey stick, just in case

—and riding kit, because of the Dartmoor ponies. Oh, and climbing things—I went to Switzerland last year, you know—and Daddy's alpenstock, and my camera, and a swim suit——"

Georgie was laughing helplessly.

"I'd like to see you catch a pony, especially in the spring. They've got foals now, you see—the sweetest little things, but the mothers won't let one go near them. But we're going to hire a cob from one of the farms for you and Patience, though he'll seem heavy-going after Aggie, I'm afraid."

Black Agnes was Susan's own mare, now stabled at the Grange, which had originally been a riding school. Patience, whose home was only two miles away from it, told them that she had visited the stables several times during the past fortnight. Georgie, who did not ride as yet, was as eager to hear all the news as Susan. She asked after Penelope, her own little brown donkey which her Uncle Archie had given her as a joke.

"Oh, she's fine," said Patience. "She was pulling the mowing machine. The grass courts are looking marvellous already. Maxwell let me feed all the horses, even Mademoiselle. I went for a ride on the General, but he doesn't much care for a side-saddle."

Her guardian allowed her to ride, but insisted that she did so in the manner of the past, in a black habit, which suited her, though it made her feel very conspicuous.

"Did you bring your kit with you?" asked Susan. "No? Oh, well, perhaps Mrs. Kane will lend you a black dressing gown. What's that you've got, Georgie? Chocolate—oh, goody, I *do* think it was a brilliant wheeze, your coming to meet us at Fontayne."

She munched with gusto. Patience accepted a small

square, and nibbled it. Georgie glanced at her sympathetically, guessing how she felt.

"Our boxroom's like a cupboard," she said, "and we're going to squeeze Sue in there every night with a shoe horn, and get her out in the morning with a tin opener. You're sleeping in our old playroom. Patience, which leads out of the bedroom which Gerry and I share. She always goes to sleep the minute she gets into bed, so we'll be able to talk."

"I'll come and talk too," said Susan. "You know, I think Gerry needs waking up. I haven't met her yet, of course, but it *can't* be healthy for a cousin of yours to be so good!"

"Oh, Gerry's all right," Georgie put in loyally, "and anyway, she'll be away part of next week. It's lucky, because Teepoo'll be coming then for two nights, and she'll be able to have Gerry's bed. Let's start collecting your things now—Driscoe's the next stop."

Patience's modest hold-all and Susan's multifarious cases, boxes and parcels were duly piled up, and the train drew to a standstill. It was a fairly small station, and Patience knew at once that the three boys waiting there must be Georgie's brothers. Her heart leapt in fear, and then calmed down as she saw their faces.

Peter, the eldest, who would be seventeen next week, had been an invalid for two years, and still had to walk with a stick, though he was much stronger now. He was tall, with a humorous, intelligent face. Even Patience could not picture Peter Kane balancing water jugs on doors, putting holly in people's beds, or indulging in any other kind of horseplay. But she was not so sure about the twins. Rough and Tough—or Ralph and Tony, to give them their real names—were short and stocky and looked young for their age. Both had wide grins and eyes that gleamed with fun.

They were accompanied by two young spaniels, who yelped excitedly at the train.

"Velvet and Plush!" cried Susan, who loved dogs, and she made a bee line for them, quite forgetting about her luggage, which Peter helped Georgie and Patience to get out. The spaniels jumped at Susan with shrill barks of pleasure, and their owners smiled approvingly at Georgie's sensible friend.

Mr. and Mrs. Kane and Gerry were waiting with the car in the station yard. When a porter had been found to cope with the luggage, and the spaniels' leads had been disentangled from the fishing rods of a fierce old gentleman who did *not* like dogs, the cavalcade marched off the platform.

"He won't bite," Rough said to Patience, seeing her draw back a little as the exuberant Plush made a sudden feint in her direction.

"Oh, I'm sure he won't. I didn't think he would, but I'm not used to dogs——"

"You don't have pets at home, then?" said the boy, to make conversation.

"We have a canary," she answered timidly, quite expecting that he would look contemptuous. But his face lit up.

"Grand—d'you think you could teach me their trill? I'm rather keen on birds, but we can't keep any because of Georgie's cat. But I'm swotting up bird calls for an entertainment-thing at St. John's, our school——"

"If you wake up in the night," Tough said to Patience, "and hear a whistling kettle boiling at gale force, that'll be Rough swotting bird calls."

She laughed. It was all right. They might tease, but they would never be unkind. She looked at their nice, friendly faces with such interest that she was thereafter able to do something which few people outside the

Kane family could do. She was always able to tell which twin was which.

Mr. and Mrs. Kane greeted their guests very warmly, and Geraldine, a fair-haired, rather supercilious-looking girl, said the correct things without the slightest sign of welcome. She looked at the girls appraisingly, noting the beautiful cut of Susan's brown tweed suit, and the extreme shagginess of the red head that surmounted it. Then her cool blue eyes travelled to Patience, and she had a disagreeable surprise. This girl was as fair as herself—but far prettier. Even in these antiquated clothes there was something distinguished about Patience, who carried herself so well and did everything with an unconscious air of dignity.

"So this is the new car that Georgie told me about in her letter," Susan exclaimed, in the station yard. "A Lodestar Ten—how *very* lucky! Uncle James has one, and I can drive it—almost——"

"Well, jump in," Mr. Kane said briskly, taking care to put her at the back. "There'll be plenty of room for everyone, as the boys and the dogs are going back with one of the farmers who lives near us. It's market day, as you can see by the stalls."

The little town of Driscoe looked very gay as the car picked its way down the narrow streets. The three girls from the Grange exchanged smiles of satisfaction. Gerry looked straight ahead.

"How gorgeous the air is!" cried Susan, who had come from London. She sniffed loudly. "It's smashing to be here, Mrs. Kane, instead of with Uncle James—though he has improved a bit, I must say. He says *I* have—he says I'm not nearly such an iggeramus as I used to be, and I told him it was because of Georgie. And then he said, 'Well, if she's managed to teach *you* anything, she must have the makings of a lion-tamer.'"

And that's a t'rrific compliment, coming from Uncle James."

Mr. and Mrs. Kane were too much astonished by this sidelight on their daughter's character to express the gratification which Susan evidently expected. Gerry sniggered.

"There's a travelling circus coming next week," she said. "I believe they've got some lions, so you can start practising. Georgie."

"No fear. King Toby's the only lion I want," Georgie returned good-humouredly. Gerry was trying to be pleasant, though as usual there was a little sting in her words. Gerry Holden, who was really a model girl in that she never forgot things, or left her room untidy, or fell into any of the normal scrapes, nevertheless lacked the right touch when it came to dealing with other people. She had been at her boarding school, St. Monica's, for years, but had made no close friends. She spent all her holidays at Wychwood, the Kanes' home, as her people were abroad; but although Georgie and her brothers were quite fond of her and took her presence for granted, they would not have minded in the least if she had chosen to go elsewhere. Until a little while ago, Gerry had looked down on Georgie, who was careless and dreamy, and had not done very well at the Driscoe High School. But now it was different. Georgie had had a term at the Grange, and had distinguished herself in various ways apart from making friends. Gerry would not have owned, even to herself, that she resented this, but she did.

"Circus?" said Mr. Kane, as they left the environs of Driscoe, and sped along the hilly moorland road that led to Dockleford. "I don't think we've heard about this——"

"Oh, yes, dear, I have. Farmer Leadbetter told me, when I went to see him yesterday to ask about hiring that cob for the girls. It's only a very small affair, staying only one night in each village," Mrs. Kane explained, well aware that her husband disliked performing animals, and might say that the family shouldn't go.

"I do hope it's on while Teepoo's here," said Georgie, and then remembered that Gerry would be away.

"Oh, don't bother about me," said her cousin, as Georgie began to say something, "I don't care for circuses, unless they're proper ones at Olympia, but I'm sure you're black friend will be thrilled to bits."

Teepoo, who was at the Grange with Georgie, Susan and Patience, was an African girl who was studying in order to become a doctor. Mr. Kane, recently returned from Africa, had met her father, so that in a way she was already a family friend. Nobody approved of Gerry's speech, which was received with silence. Susan, whose temper matched her fiery hair, disliked Georgie's cousin from that moment.

They were passing through a pretty little village, and now Georgie was able to point out a house just showing through the trees.

"Here we are. That's home. There's King Toby, waiting for us on the dining-room window sill. . . ."

Wychwood was a most attractive house, with a lovely garden now full of spring flowers. Susan, whose parents were wealthy and gave her everything she could possibly want, except a settled home, looked at it with delight, and Patience was silent, mentally comparing it with the dismal old ruin where she lived with her guardian.

"Run along in, all of you," laughed Mrs. Kane. "Let's leave the luggage till afterwards. There are potato cakes for tea, and I can see Mrs. Duncan signalling to say they're ready."

The four girls all very much of an age, but each so different in outlook and upbringing, went quickly into the house. Mr. and Mrs. Kane followed more slowly.

"Well, talk about mixed bags," said Georgie's father, as he knocked out his pipe against the veranda rail. "I prophesy an exciting wind-up to the holidays. I feel certain that Miss Susan Walker will see to that."

"Yes, she *is* lively," Mrs. Kane agreed, "but how nice to think she's really learnt something from Georgie, who used to be so shy. Poor Patience is shy now, but in another way. She must be an orphan, I suppose. I do hope they'll all settle down happily together. Really, with three boys in the house and four girls, it's like having a school of our own. . . ."

Peter, Rough, and Tough now emerged from a farmer's car which had stopped by the gate, and five minutes later peace reigned at Wychwood as its hungry inhabitants settled down to a belated tea.

CHAPTER TWO

SOMETHING LOST

GEORGIE smuggled King Toby up to bed with her that night. This beautiful orange cat was her especial joy and pride, and in his own solemn way he made it quite evident that he returned her affection. Like many of his kind, however, he was apt to be jealous, and she saw that he was not pleased by the arrival of Susan and Patience. That was why she captured him when she met him on the stairs, and carried him into the bedroom while Gerry was having her bath.

Now Gerry was asleep, her plaits draped neatly on the pillow, and Toby was purring softly on Georgie's eiderdown, while from the adjoining playroom there came small, restless sounds as though Patience were trying to settle down, and couldn't.

Georgie whispered her name at last, and a slender figure in a long white nightdress appeared instantly in the doorway.

"What is it, Georgie?"

"Nothing. I just wondered how you were. I couldn't come and see, because I've got King Toby, and he doesn't like being disturbed. Aren't you sleepy?"

"Not very," Patience answered, sitting on the edge of the bed, and stroking the drowsy cat.

"A strange house is horrid, just at first," said Georgie, very sorry for her. "I know what you feel like——"

"You don't." Patience spoke in a desperate little whisper, quite unlike her usually sedate tones. "No one can possibly know. You see, I've never even been inside a real home before, let alone stayed in one. . . . It makes me feel—odd."

Georgie remembered now that Patience had spoken very little about her own concerns, and had never been heard to mention her parents, who had presumably died years ago.

"It's a pity you couldn't have stayed in a quieter home to start with," she said sympathetically, "but you'll get used to it. The family like you awfully—I could see that at once. Don't you—don't you remember your own people at all?"

Patience shook her head.

"Georgie, I'll tell you a secret. Miss Primrose knows, but nobody else at the Grange. I don't even know who my people were. Guardie will never talk about them. I don't know if I'm related to him or not—or where I was born, or anything. He says I'll know all in good time; that his lawyers will tell me if he dies before I'm twenty-one—as he quite likely may," said poor Patience, "as he's ninety-three and I'm only thirteen. . . ."

"You mean you've no aunts or uncles or cousins? And you don't know who your father was, or when he died, or what he did? And you can't remember your mother——?" Georgie could hardly grasp such a state of desolation.

"I do remember her," said Patience. She looked away, and the moonlight played softly on her long fair hair. "I didn't think I did until to-night. Then when your mother kissed me goodnight, I remembered someone else doing the same thing, years and years ago—only she was much taller than your mother, or perhaps that was because I must have been very little. . . ."

Patience's voice shook for a moment, but she soon recovered herself.

"There must be lots of people in the same boat, and I'm lucky to have got Guardie, because he's a perfect dear even if he does think that everything modern is awful. Don't look so worried, Georgie. I'm used to it, and I don't usually mind—only coming here and seeing you all together——"

"I simply can't imagine having no family, and not even knowing——" Georgie broke off. There was no point in rubbing it into Patience that she was in a very peculiar position. "Well, you'll have to go shares in *my* family, that's all, and," she said heroically, "you can borrow King Toby for a start."

"Oh, no, I couldn't possibly take him away from you," said Patience, who had never slept with a cat in her life, and didn't much want to begin. But Georgie was in a self-sacrificing mood, and would not be gainsaid.

"Yes, you must—just for to-night. To make you feel at home, you know. I say, we'd better go to sleep now, because there'll be lots to do to-morrow."

Patience agreed with this. She felt much less lonely now that she had told Georgie her sad little secret, and her heart was light as she gathered up the sleepy form of King Toby and conveyed him to her own room. She found the rhythmic purring very soothing, and was fast asleep herself within two minutes.

It was a warm night, however, and Toby was no lightweight. Patience dreamed that she was wearing an orange-coloured feather boa that was really a hot-water bottle, and woke up panting. She shifted her companion and slept again, to waken this time to the sound of horses' hooves and heavy, trundling wheels. Something soft flicked her cheek—Toby's tail—and a gentle thud told her that he had jumped on to the carpet. Perhaps he wanted to see what mysterious traffic was passing along this moorland road by night. She thought she would like to see it too—but somehow she dropped off to sleep again, and next time she opened her eyes it was morning, and Georgie was in the doorway saying that it was time to get up.

The whole family met at breakfast, which was a hilarious meal. Rough and Tough were going to take the spaniels for a long walk; Peter and his father had arranged to play a few holes at the small golf course nearby, and Georgie and Gerry were to take the two guests down to Valley Farm, to inspect the stout cob which Mr. Leadbetter had promised to lend them if they liked.

"But we can't all go out and leave you alone, Mrs. Kane," Susan exclaimed, as she worked her way happily through a large country breakfast. "I'll stay with you, shall I? I could help, you know, with the cooking. I can make meringues and fudge."

Gerry snorted, but Mrs. Kane thanked Susan for the offer.

"Meringues would be lovely for tea one day, Susan.

Let's keep them up our sleeves for the next rainy afternoon. But Mrs. Duncan will help me this morning, and I particularly want you and Patience to have some riding while you're here. If you come next holidays, it will be easier, because I suppose Spot will be installed by then."

Spot—who was spotless, by the way—was Teepoo's horse, which she had insisted upon giving to Georgie. He was at the Grange at present, as Georgie couldn't ride yet, but the whole Kane clan was longing for his advent.

"Farmer Leadbetter's cob is an awful-looking thing," Gerry said disdainfully.

"Do you ride?" Susan asked fiercely.

"No, but——"

"Do you mean you don't, or you can't? Because if you've had no experience, you can't be much of a judge," said Susan, who was thorough in everything —particularly her dislikes.

"I don't pretend to be a judge of horses. I don't want to be," said Gerry, in her haughtiest tone. "But I have had lots of experience in other things. For instance, I can think of a more sensible menu for lunch than meringues and fudge——"

Rough uttered a small miaou which everyone refused to hear.

"Look at the time, Georgie," said Mrs. Kane. "I told Mr. Leadbetter you'd be at the farm at ten."

"Yes, Mother, we'll put a girdle round the earth in forty minutes," cried Georgie, leaping up. She had literary leanings and was apt to plunge into quotations at any moment.

"You mean a bridle," said Susan, who scarcely knew what a quotation was. She saw Gerry's superior smile, and looked at Rough, encouraged by that little miaou of his which nobody had remarked upon. "By the way, where's King Toby?" she asked, as she folded up her table napkin.

Georgie had been wondering the same thing, and looked inquiringly at her mother.

"He left me some time during the night," said Patience. "I don't know when, but it was still dark."

"You had him in bed with you?" Gerry looked shocked. "Aunt Marcia doesn't like cats upstairs."

"Oh, I don't worry unduly—it's only that Georgie would take him up every night if I didn't put my foot down, and I don't think it's good for either of them," Mrs. Kane explained, feeling that she would like to spank her officious niece. "Now run along, all of you. Toby'll come home presently for his breakfast."

It was a pretty walk along field paths to Valley Farm, which was an old house built in the Devonshire style, beamed heavily in black oak, and deeply thatched. Georgie hardly knew Farmer Leadbetter or his busy wife and family, for until she went away to school she had been too shy to make friends locally, She braced herself to meet them to-day, but the yard was empty. Susan whistled "There's nobody home but us chickens", as some feathered forms squawked and fluttered indignantly in the hedge.

"Well, there's the cob, anyway," said Gerry, indicating an old wooden stable from which came sounds of whinnying and stamping. "He doesn't sound very sweet-tempered, does he?"

"He's just impatient," said Susan, and went up to the door.

"Let's find Mr. Leadbetter first," said Georgie, looking round the deserted yard. "Mother thought he was expecting us."

"Oh, he's forgotten, I suppose. I *say*," exclaimed Susan, as she opened the top half of the stable door.

"What a wizard horse! This isn't a cob, Gerry. There's some Arab blood in him—isn't there, Georgie? You must have seen him about?"

All this time Susan was stroking the sensitive black muzzle which the occupant of the stable had thrust over the door. She looked astonished when Georgie had to confess that she had never noticed this particular horse.

"They all looked alike to me before I went to the Grange," she said wryly. "I expect I *have* seen him, but——"

"From a safe distance," Gerry murmured, sitting down on a convenient mounting block. "Well, isn't someone going to saddle him? It's getting quite late."

"I'll go to the house and see if Mr. Leadbetter's there," said Georgie, and ran across the yard and through the garden gate.

"Have a biscuit, you beauty," said Susan, who had come well supplied with titbits, as usual. She crumbled the biscuit for the horse, who took a piece languidly, and then leaned his head against her.

"Do look, Patience—he's like a lamb. I could take him out bareback," said Susan, stroking the thick mane.

She had no intention of doing this, and would not have gone so far as to unfasten the lower door if Gerry had not chipped in.

"You're not to touch him until Farmer Leadbetter's said it's all right. Why, you said yourself that it wasn't a cob—this may not be the right one."

"Oh, Gerry, don't," whispered Patience. "Don't tell her she mustn't—that's the very worst thing to do with Sue. Here you are, Susan—I brought half an apple. He may like it better than biscuits."

"You're not to feed him, either," said Gerry, and that was really too much.

"Have a biscuit, you beauty."

"You go and find the farmer yourself," flared Susan, "and tell him I'll be back for lunch!"

She had got the door open by this time. The black horse came sidling out, looking rather bewildered. Susan, grasping his mane, sprang on to his back. She was wonderfully agile, and often mounted her own Black Agnes this way.

"Bravo," cried Patience.

"Swank," sniffed Gerry. "She ought to come to St. Monica's for a term or two——"

The rest of her words were lost in the dreadful crash that neither girl ever forgot. The horse, after taking a few staggering steps, had suddenly collapsed, bringing Susan down with him to the cobbled surface of the yard.

Susan was thrown clear, and, characteristically, her first thought was for the animal.

"Oh, Paish, he's hurt—he can't get up. Go and get help from somewhere—yes, yes, I'm perfectly all right."

She wasn't, though. Her freckled face was slowly turning green, and blood was beginning to soak through one sleeve. As Patience, terrified, turned towards the farmhouse, Susan quietly fainted.

"Now, now, what's all this?" cried a new voice, and Patience saw the burly figure of the farmer approaching, with Georgie at his side. When he saw the fallen horse, his face lost its ruddy hue, and he muttered something between his teeth.

"Let me help you get him up," pleaded Patience, as Georgie ran to Susan. Gerry had already taken off her own jacket and was rolling it into a pillow.

"Nay, leave him be, miss," said the farmer. "Reckon this will be the end of poor old Jet. He was sick, see—I'd put him by himself till Mr. Jones, the vet, could get out here to see him."

The horse struggled feebly and lay still. Patience tried to speak again, but there was too big a lump in her throat.

"Off you go, all of you," said Mr. Leadbetter. "Is your friend coming round, Miss Kane? I'll carry her, shall I? I've got to come indoors—to get my gun."

Georgie looked at the horse, and a lump came into her throat too. She wondered what poor Susan would say, when she realised what had happened.

"I told them not to," said Gerry.

"A mighty lot of use saying that now," growled the farmer, looking down at Susan's limp body in his arms. He fancied he saw her eyelids twitch. "There's no blame to anyone," he said firmly.

But Susan had recovered, and now she gazed at him in sickening anxiety.

"The horse——?"

"Now don't you fret, missie—" began the man.

"It's got to be shot," said Gerry.

Susan closed her eyes again, very tightly indeed, but tears forced their way through her lashes. The farmer laid her on a shiny sofa in his parlour, and his wife and grown-up daughter brought bandages and a bowl of water.

"There, there, my dearie, don't cry—there's no bones broken," said Mrs. Leadbetter, as she skilfully cut away the blood-stained sleeve.

"I know there aren't. I wish there were. I'd rather break my own bones than—than know I'd killed the horse. And I'm not crying, anyway, so there!" choked Susan, with a startling disregard for truth.

"Old Jet was ill," said the the daughter, whose name was Connie. "We all thought he'd have to go—though I was hoping we could keep him in the lower meadow for a pet, like. We're all powerful fond of him. But 'tisn't your fault—it's Dad's, if it's anyone's, or mine, because there should have been someone to meet you in the yard. Only we've been that deeved this morning——"

"Oh, excuse me, but I've just seen Mr. Jones arriving," Georgie said quickly, making for the door. "I'll call Mr. Leadbetter at once, in case he shoots."

And by a lucky chance she was just in time to save the horse, as the farmer was raising his gun when she dashed into the yard.

"Mr. Jones here, Miss Kane? That's good news. Run away now like a good lass—your friends are downalong the orchard," he said, as he naturally wished the girls out of the way.

So Georgie joined Patience and Gerry, who were prowling gloomily amongst the blossoming trees. Even Gerry was sorry about the horse, though she did not feel for Susan as the other two did.

"*What* a beginning to your visit," she said to Patience. "Let's hope nothing more will happen, anyway . . ."

"Perhaps something nice will," said Georgie, with a forlorn gulp.

A few moments later, to her great surprise, something nice did happen—for Connie Leadbetter came to find them, a smile on her round, fresh face.

"Mum says, will you all come in and have some cocoa. Your friend's arm's stopped bleeding now, and Mr. Jones has told Dad that old Jet don't need to be put down this time! Yes, we can pull him round, and though maybe he won't work again, we can keep him till winter anyway. Maybe you think it's queer for a farmer's daughter to be so set on an animal—but Jet was my brother's, see, and he was killed in the war. I was a mite at the time, but Tom Mayne was a pupil here then, and he taught me to ride Jet."

"I know how you feel," said Georgie, "because

I've got a cat. I've got a horse too, now, and a donkey—and I love them, but I don't think they'll ever come up to King Toby."

"He's the yellow cat, isn't he? Tom says he catches rats in his barn," smiled Connie. She was engaged to Tom Mayne now, and his small but flourishing farm abutted the garden at Wychwood. "Now just you go into the parlour, and I'll bring the cocoa, and mind you tell your friend that Jet's spared."

Of course they told Susan that—Georgie and Patience shouted the good news in unison, and saw the distress on the freckled face change to relief.

"Aye, we'll keep the old chap till winter," Connie assured her, as she brought in cups and saucers, a large spiced cake, and a steaming jug.

"Why only till winter? Can't you take him in and give him hay, if you can't get corn?" demanded Susan.

Connie looked at her mother, and smiled rather sadly.

"We will if we can. But it's hard enough to feed the working horses," she said. "Times are bad."

"They always are, for farmers," Gerry said dispassionately. She had no intention of being rude, but spoke with her usual disregard for other people's feelings. "The weather, or something, is always wrong. But you've got such heaps of hay—you could surely feed the horse if you're so fond of him."

"Our hay don't get wasted, Miss, for all we get so much. We have to sell," Mrs. Leadbetter said sharply, annoyed by the girl's critical attitude. "Connie here would keep all the old horses if she could, she's that soft, but poor folks can't do that kind of thing. 'Be just before you're generous'—that's what I say."

"Are you hard up, then?" cried Susan, starting up in alarm. "Oh dear, and I've had three slices of cake——"

They couldn't help laughing at that, and Connie explained that things were not so desperate that they had to grudge their visitors food.

"We're no worse off than most," she said staunchly, "but Mum's upset by what happened this morning. Someone broke in here last night and took a cash-box that had over twenty pounds in it. Dad sold some calves yesterday for cash, and left the money out."

"So that's why he wasn't there to meet us, and why you were all deeved," said Susan, who had taken a fancy to the last word. "Twenty pounds— how awful."

"Who could have taken it?" asked Georgie, horrified.

"Gipsies, maybe. We can't prove it, so we can't say it; but the police think the same. There was a lot of them passed through last night," said Connie.

"That must be what I heard," said Patience. "How terrible for you—I do hope you'll get it back."

"Not much hope of that," sighed Mrs. Leadbetter; and then Connie took the girls to see Candy, the fat old cob intended for their use, and saw them off the premises.

"Come again whenever you like," she said, "though you'd better let that cut heal before you try out any more tricks." That injunction was for Susan, who hung her head. "Good-bye, my dears, and keep out of mischief."

Mrs. Kane was looking somewhat preoccupied when the chastened girls returned to Wychwood. She examined Susan's arm, and agreed that the Leadbetters had behaved very kindly, and she heartily seconded Connie's hope that the girls would steer clear of further trouble.

After lunch she called Georgie aside.

"Darling, there's something I must tell you," she said sorrowfully. "Toby hasn't been in all morning, and—Mrs. Duncan says that her husband saw him early in the day, in the arms of a gipsy child. The child was in a caravan, crossing the moor, heading for Periton. Daddy has rung up the police, and the Lads are going off on their bicycles to try to catch up the caravans. But I'm afraid—you see, the scent's cold now, Georgie, and I'm afraid we shan't see King Toby again."

CHAPTER THREE

UPHEAVALS

GEORGIE stared at her mother in mingled horror and bewilderment.

"But—why didn't Mr. Duncan rescue him?" she gasped. "He'll be *miles* away by now. . . ."

"He wasn't sure that it was Toby, darling, till Mrs. Duncan mentioned that he was missing. Of course, he *may* be mistaken—but I'm afraid not. You must be brave about it," said Mrs. Kane, "and remember that you've got two guests to look after."

"Yes, but—oh, mother, King Toby! I can't believe that we'll never see him again. What time did Mr. Duncan see him?" Georgie asked unsteadily. "The Leadbetters had some money stolen in the night, and they think the gipsies took that."

"I expect it was the same caravan," said her mother, "because he met them when he was going to work, and he starts very early. Now what about taking up these magazines for Susan to read?"

Susan, much to her disgust, had been persuaded to lie down that afternoon, and Georgie accordingly went up to see her. Patience was with her, and they both looked so forlorn that Georgie realized that she must put her own feelings aside now and entertain her friends. So she fetched some sweets, and they all chattered for some time; and then Patience asked if Toby had come home yet.

Georgie had to tell them what had happened, and how the twins had rushed off on their bicycles as soon as they heard the news. The girls were almost as upset as she was herself, and Patience, with a stab of self-reproach, said that if only she hadn't let Toby escape in the night, it would never have happened.

"That's simply silly. You know what cats are—if they feel like going out; and the windows are open, they just *go,*" said Georgie. "Perhaps he wanted to see what was passing. It must have been getting on for dawn, and I suppose they saw him and—took him, before going on to Valley Farm."

"They were heading for Periton, you said," mused Susan. "Where's that? Very far away?"

"Twelve miles. Rough and Tough ought to catch them up long before they get there—if they *are* going there: but there are heaps of turnings off the Periton road, leading to all the little villages, and they may be going to one of those."

"Georgie! I know," said Patience excitedly, "let me go back to the farm and borrow Candy, and I'll follow. I might be able to help the boys if there's any trouble. . . ."

There she sat on the foot of Susan's bed, a slender figure in her prim, old-fashioned frock, with her long fair braids hanging demurely down her back. Georgie tried—and failed—to picture her bearding a band of truculent gipsies.

"You'd get lost," she said. "You don't know the moor at all. But thanks for thinking of it, though. Well—it's happened, and whining won't help. I'm afraid your visit hasn't started off very well, but let's hope that nothing else will spoil it."

"I wish I could get that money back for the Leadbetters," sighed Susan. "They were so frightfully decent about Jet. I wonder if Daddy——?"

"Oh, no," Georgie cut in quickly, "they wouldn't take anything from him, or anybody else. Of course, it would be different if we could get their *own* twenty pounds back. How I wish I could ride! If I could, I'd borrow some kind of a horse, and Paish could have Candy, as she said, and we'd both go after them. By the way, 'Paish' is pretty awful, isn't it, Patience? Shall we call you Pat?"

The fair girl smiled rather constrainedly, and later on, when she and Georgie were in the garden, holding one end of the tennis net while Peter tried to tighten it, she returned to the subject.

"Guardie doesn't like nicknames, and he's very particular about my being called Patience, so please always call me that."

"All right. I don't know why Sue and I started 'Paish'—it's hideous," said Georgie. "I suppose your guardian named you Patience himself?"

"No, it's my real name—the only thing that really belongs to me. When I first came to him, that was the only thing I could say. That's all he's ever told me. . . . Oh, here are Rough and Tough. They haven't found King Toby."

One glance at the twins' downcast faces was sufficient to tell that they had failed in their quest for King Toby.

"We didn't even see the gipsies," groaned Rough, throwing himself full-length on the grass. "Am I stiff! We got as far as Periton, but we promised Dad we'd turn around at four o'clock—so we had to. We've asked no end of people if they'd seen any caravans, but they hadn't. Poor old Toby may be absolutely anywhere on the moor. Perhaps he's one of those cats who can travel for miles and miles to get home."

Georgie smiled faintly, but she knew as well as he did that her pet had led far too protected a life to show such self-reliance. The whole family had spoilt him, and he had never been more than a short distance away from the house.

"We met Tom Mayne as we were coming in," said Tough. "Leading a brown pony. He got him at Driscoe market yesterday, and has just been to fetch him. He's to be a present for Miss Leadbetter. Tom's keeping him for a few days, so I told him you'd like to have a look, Patience. We can go this evening if you like."

"Oh, yes," beamed Patience. "Georgie, do you think Sue can come too?"

Mrs. Kane, however, thought that Susan was safer where she was, so Patience went off with the twins after supper, for the April evenings were growing longer now, and Georgie and Peter played three-handed cribbage with the indignant invalid. Gerry had gone out by herself, as she did sometimes.

"One for his nob," said Susan. "I mean, two for his heels. Oh, *bother* his nob and his heels—I shall never learn this game. Why can't the police catch those gipsies? Even if they wouldn't do it for a cat, surely they might try to get back the Leadbetters' money?"

"It's not as easy as you think," said Peter, beginning to build a card house, now that the half-hearted game was over. "For one thing, there's no proof that gipsies did take that money—it might have been picked up by any tramp. As for Toby, there's no actual proof there either, and even if there were—you couldn't get police to put a cordon round Dartmoor to find one stolen cat."

"Is Gerry in here?" asked Mrs. Kane, looking round the door.

"No, Mother, she went for a walk," said Georgie. "It's late, though. Patience and the Lads came back some time ago. Oh, here she is now—Gerry, you're terribly late, my dear. You mustn't stay out so long," Mrs. Kane told her errant niece, who answered with her usual coolness.

"Sorry, Auntie. I had to ring up a friend."

"We met Tom Mayne as we were coming in."

"But you've been out—you haven't been using the 'phone."

"I went to the call-box on the other side of Dockleford," Gerry explained loftily, and went to take off her coat.

Susan pulled a face at Georgie, who couldn't help smiling, though Peter, she noticed, pretended not to see the grimace. Just before bedtime, Mrs. Kane called Georgie into the kitchen and shut the door.

"Don't leave Gerry out of things, will you?" she began. "I sometimes think she feels odd man out here. I know it isn't always easy, especially when you've got

Sue and Patience, but remember to be nice to Gerry too."

Georgie didn't say "She isn't nice to us," because she knew that her mother was well aware of the fact, and, moreover, always refused to listen to anything in the nature of tale-bearing. But she didn't see why the niceness should be all on one side.

At bedtime, however, she did try to coax her cousin to join in the conversation she was having with Patience, upon the vexed question of circuses. Patience, who had never been to one, said they were cruel and oughtn't to be allowed. Georgie, who had sat enthralled more than once under the Big Top, insisted that the animals liked it. Hadn't she seen a dear little chimp on a bicycle clapping his own hands with glee as the audience applauded?

"*I* don't know if the animals like it or not," said Gerry. "I'm bored to a frenzy as a rule, unless it's awfully well done. Last time my people were in England, we went to a marvellous one in London. I remember there was a cat on a tight-rope, and it had to jump into a sort of—sorry, Georgie, I'd forgotten about poor old Toby."

"Forgotten him—oh, Gerry! I was just thinking—how frightful if the gipsies sell him to a circus! He was so good at jumping," said poor Georgie, as—like Barbara Allen's spineless sweetheart—she turned her face "unto the wall".

"They couldn't train him at his age, idiot. They have to start as kittens," Gerry said gruffly, but it was obvious that she was only trying to cover up her tactlessness. Georgie said no more, and silence fell—until Patience had her brainwave.

"When we were coming from Driscoe yesterday," she said suddenly, "didn't someone mention that a circus was coming here?"

"Next week," said Georgie. "A little travelling one—— Oh, you don't think——?"

"Well, no. Not really," Patience admitted. "I don't think circuses want cats—except that he's so beautiful. I just wondered——"

"*I'm* wondering how anyone can get to sleep with all this nattering going on," growled Gerry, making her bed creak angrily.

"Yes, we must go to sleep," agreed Patience, before Georgie could find a cutting retort. "We'll have a busy day to-morrow, looking for King Toby."

At breakfast next morning, however, there were other things to think about. The postman had called earlier than usual, and Peter caught Georgie's arm just as she was going into the dining-room.

"Mother's heard from Pencarne. Great-Grannie's ill. Uncle Archie says he doesn't think it's serious, but Mother's worried. And Daddy's in a flap too, about a cable he's had—he'll tell you about it. Anyway, they've had breakfast by themselves, and you're to sit in Mother's place now and pour out the tea."

Georgie did this, explaining her parents' absence to Susan and Patience.

"I remember your telling Guardie about your great-grandparents," remarked the latter. "I do hope everything will be all right."

"Oh, so do I—they're so sweet," said Georgie. "They had their golden wedding just before I came to the Grange. They're Mother's grandparents, you see, and they brought her up—and her brother, who's Gerry's father—because her own father and mother died young. They live in Cornwall, at a lovely little place called Pencarne, and Uncle Archie—the one who gave me Penelope—and his wife live there too. Her mother's cousin."

"If your Great-Grannie dies, will Paish and I have

to go home?" asked Susan, direct as ever, as she polished off the last piece of toast.

"She won't die," said Gerry, with her most superior air. "It's only a slight chill. Uncle Archie said so on the 'phone last night."

"You rang *him* up?" gasped Georgie; for they were not very fond of this particular relative.

"Yes, I did. It's a free country," snapped Gerry, "and I'll go and tell Auntie that she needn't flap about Great-Grannie——"

Mrs. Kane came into the room just at that moment, so Gerry told her there and then that she had spoken to Pencarne the night before. Her aunt was naturally surprised to find that she had been so secretive about it, but the reassuring news about her grandmother came as a relief.

"The letter was posted much earlier in the day," she remarked, "so if Uncle Archie said she was better last night, she must be on the mend. I'm so glad—for another reason too. You'll all be surprised to hear that Daddy has had a cable from N'wambo."

"*Gosh,*" breathed Tough. "That's Teepoo's father, isn't it? The native chief our revered pop has stayed with. What does he want, Mother? Georgie to go to Africa for a holiday?"

"No," laughed Mrs. Kane, "he's coming to England. He arrives to-morrow. He doesn't make any demands at all, but Daddy feels he'd like to meet him and show him round London a bit, as he was entertained so well at N'wambo's home. He couldn't have gone, of course, if I'd had to go to Pencarne—but now he'll be able to."

"I suppose N'wambo will stay with Teepoo," said Georgie. "She's with English friends in London. I wonder if she'll bring him here when she comes next week?"

"If ever a house needed elastic walls, this is it," said Rough; but he looked pleased at the prospect of meeting a real African chieftain. "Wonder if he can teach me any bird-calls! What sort of birds are there in his part of the world, Peter?"

"Parrots," said Tough, before their elder brother could speak, "and you don't want anyone to teach you what *they* sound like. . . . If Daddy's going to London to-day, he might take us in to Driscoe with him, and we could put an advertisement in the local rag for Toby."

They all thought this a splendid idea. Georgie said she would offer a reward for his safe return. Mr. Kane decided to travel up to London by the midday train, and spend the night at his club, so he took the twins and Georgie into Driscoe by car, leaving it at a garage until he should return.

Susan and Patience, left behind with Mrs. Kane and Gerry, jumped at the chance of having a ride.

"I've spoken to Mr. Mayne, my dears, and he's quite willing for one of you to ride his new pony," announced Mrs. Kane. "His name is Timbo, and he's very steady. Yes, Susan, I quite appreciate the meaning of your lifted brow, but you must remember that while you're here I'm responsible for you, and you can do your steeplechasing elsewhere. So why not collect Timbo and then go over to Valley Farm for Candy, and have a ride on the moor?"

"I haven't a habit," Patience murmured, "and I don't expect anyone's got a side-saddle. . . ."

"*Can't* you ride astride?" asked Peter.

"Oh, yes, I have done so—Guardie hasn't forbidden me, but he always says it's so hoydenish——"

"Up, the hoydens!" said Susan. "I'll lend you my jodhpurs and a sweater, and wear my shorts. Unless Peter or the Lads have got anything better."

They hadn't, but Connie Leadbetter, who was not very tall, was able to lend Susan some nice cord breeches and a coat.

"Keep them as long as you like," she said kindly. "I'm not likely to want them yet awhile."

"But aren't you simply *aching* to try Timbo?" cried Susan.

"Reckon I'll have to ache," was Connie's dry response, "seeing every hand's needed on the farm. There, now," she went on, as both girls began to speak, "I might have known you'd be offering help. Thank you both, I'm sure, but it's skilled help we want. . . . Just you go out and enjoy yourselves, and no more accidents!"

Susan grinned sheepishly. She had already taken a piece of long-cherished chocolate to Jet, who was wonderfully better to-day. The farmer said that chocolate couldn't hurt him, and Susan thought it had done him good.

"I do like Timbo," she said to Patience, who was riding the sturdy Candy, and looking very trim in Susan's clothes.

The brown pony turned his head and whinnied softly, as if he appreciated the compliment. Susan patted his glossy neck.

"I wish Connie Leadbetter didn't have to work so hard," she went on sadly. Hard work was one of her own nightmares, which made her all the more sympathetic. "Oh, Paish, if only we could get that money back from the gipsies . . . and Georgie's King Toby too."

"I've been thinking and thinking about that," said Patience, reining in as they came to the edge of the moor—a mass of glowing colours to-day, in the clear light of spring. "Oh, Sue, isn't it lovely? Look at all those paths—going in different directions. I didn't know there was so *much* of Dartmoor. I've been picturing it like the common at home."

"That little common at Lennet Magna? Patience!"

"Well, I haven't been about much," Patience defended herself. "One could get lost here. . . . Don't let's go out of sight of the road."

"All right. We'll just go as far as that little hill and back. Oh, I beg its pardon—Georgie says hills are *tors* in these parts. Come on—we'll walk, I think, in case of rabbit holes." Susan, having uttered the most prudent speech of her life, made Timbo step across the springy heather to the path that led to the tor.

It was farther than they thought—when they had had a longer acquaintance with Dartmoor, they came to understand how deceptive distance can be—but it was a lovely morning, and Mrs. Kane, surely the easiest of hostesses, had told them that lunch would be cold, and it didn't matter if they were late.

"It's tons bigger than I thought," said Susan, referring to the tor, which loomed above them in quite an impressive manner as they approached it. "And it's so rocky—I don't know if Timbo would care to climb up it."

"Candy wants to—I expect he's done it before," laughed Patience, as the cob, treading daintily, began to pick his way through the loose rocks.

Timbo, not to be outdone, followed suit. They could not reach the top of the tor, but stood on a broad plateau about half way up, while their riders exclaimed with delight at the wonderful view.

"It's like looking half across the world. There's a village over there—where the smoke is—and what looks like a river beyond——" Susan was shading her eyes against the sun. "Or *is* it a village?" she murmured. "It looks more like—Patience, it's a gipsies' encampment. . . ."

"I believe it is, Sue—— Oh, what are you going to do?" cried Patience, as her impetuous friend urged Timbo to descend.

"Go and see if they've got Toby, and the twenty pounds——"

"Susan Walker, use your brains," Patience said severely, as Candy followed the pony at his steady, solemn pace. "That camp is miles away, and we'd lose ourselves trying to find it. The gipsies might have moved on before we got there—and in any case, *would* they be likely to give up Toby or the money to two girls? Why, before we knew it, they'd steal Candy and Timbo, and all our clothes as well!"

"What can we do, then?" wailed Susan, forced to see the wisdom of these words.

"Go back as soon as we can and tell Mrs. Kane and Peter. Georgie and the Lads may be back by now," said Patience, turning her horse.

Susan groaned, but raised no objection. They returned to the village, and hastened to Wychwood. Gerry met them at the gate.

"Georgie and the boys haven't come back yet," she said, in answer to Susan's question. "I'm going to the post office. Aunt Marcia's had to send for a relative of hers to come and look after us. She's got to go to Pencarne after all, as our great-grandmother is much worse."

It would be unfair to say that Geraldine Holden enjoyed imparting bad news, but whenever she found herself the bearer of unwelcome tidings she assumed a very busy, self-important manner which could not fail to irritate her audience.

"Pneumonia," she added wisely. "I don't suppose Great-Grannie'll get over it."

Susan dismounted and tied Timbo to the gate while she ran off in search of Mrs. Kane, whom she found at the store cupboard with Mrs. Duncan, working out meals for the forthcoming week.

"I'm awfully sorry about your grannie," said Susan, "but she may pull through. Black Aggie—that's my mare—had pneumonia *and* a strained hock last year, and she got better, and she's no chicken. And I'd like to say that Patience and I will help with the cooking while you're away. . . ."

"That's very kind of you, miss, I'm sure," said Mrs. Duncan, hiding a smile, "but I'll be able to come in every day and see to things."

"And I'm hoping that one of Georgie's aunts-by-marriage will be able to come and sleep here," added Mrs. Kane, "but it's very nice to know that you'll help. It *is* sad about my grandmother, because, although she's very old now, she's so sweet that everyone loves her, and will miss her if she doesn't get better. Georgie will be very unhappy, I'm afraid—especially as this news has come on top of King Toby's disappearance."

"Oh——" Susan opened her mouth to tell Georgie's mother about the gipsies' encampment on the moor, but she was beginning to notice other people more, and so she held her peace. Mrs. Kane's face was very white, and although she spoke so calmly, it was evident that she was very much upset.

"And it might have been only a wild goose chase after all," Susan told herself, as she heard Georgie's voice in the hall.

The family had lunch at once, as Mrs. Kane had to catch the afternoon bus into Driscoe, where she would pick up the car which her husband had garaged there only that morning. Georgie and Peter helped her to pack, while the others took Velvet and Plush for a walk.

"I won't be very long," she said, "whatever happens, because the message was that the crisis was expected soon. And I've asked Aunt Kate to come as soon as possible. She told me, that time I went over to see her, that she would always come if we wanted her."

"But we don't know her," said Georgie, appalled, "and she's only an 'in-law'—Aunt Milly's sister. Oh, sorry, Mother, I don't mean to grumble—it's just that everything seems to have gone wrong at once——"

"I know, darling. And you and Susan and Patience were going to have such a lovely time. Never mind, we'll all be together again soon, and in the meantime you must see that the girls enjoy themselves. Don't let them get depressed," cautioned Mrs. Kane. "Now, Peter, if you'd be ready to snap these locks when Georgie sits on the case. . . ."

The packing was all done. Georgie and Peter escorted their mother to the bus stop, and waved goodbye. As they drew near home, Gerry ran out to meet them, waving a telegram.

"It came the very moment we got back from our walk. Rough opened it, as Auntie'd gone. Listen," she said dramatically, and read aloud: " 'Cannot come. Decorators in house. Kate.' "

CHAPTER FOUR

ON THE TRAIL

"I THINK it's *wizard* to be all on our own," Susan observed at tea. "I don't mean to be rude, of course —Mr. and Mrs. Kane are the tops; quite the nicest parents I've ever met, next to mine. But they're grown-ups, when all's said and done, and the very best of grown-ups have to say 'Don't' sometimes. They can't help it, I suppose. We may say 'Don't' ourselves some day. . . ."

Gerry looked at her as if she would like to say it then and there, but Tough stepped into the breach.

"Peter can jolly well say it *now*. He's the skipper. There's got to be someone—er——"

"Skipping?" asked Susan sweetly.

"Someone at the helm," said Tough, "or you have mutiny and anarchy, and all the rest of it. All the same," he added, looking round the table, "this *is* rather good, I do think."

Georgie agreed, but Peter knitted his brows as he wondered whether he ought to let his parents know of this unexpected predicament. Mrs. Kane could not leave the old lady who might be dying at this very moment, but the boy knew quite well that his father would forego his meeting with N'wambo rather than leave Wychwood as it was at present. And that, thought Peter, would be a pity. Not only would the African chief's visit to London be far less pleasant, but more plans would have to be upset, as Mr. Kane had decided to look up several friends on his brief visit to London.

("And why need we worry him, when everything's under perfect control?" Peter asked himself. "We're not kids, and there are enough of us, goodness knows. . . .")

"I've got a lovely idea," said Georgie, who had been watching Peter's face, and was relieved to see that he had made up his mind. "We want it to be a decent holiday, don't we? Mother was the first to say that we must make things nice for Sue and Patience. Well, let's do something unusual every day. Let's write down a suggestion for tomorrow, and jumble them up in a hat, then Peter can take one out and we'll do it."

"H'm," said Susan. "Lucky the Kenpot can't hear you, my child. That's Miss Kennedy, the English mistress at school," she added, for the boys' information. "Still, never mind, Georgie, we understand what you mean. Yes, let's do it. Who's got a pencil?"

"Let's clear the decks first," laughed Peter, and they disposed of the remains of tea, and washed up the cups and saucers. Then they all went back to the dining-room, and the twins found pencils and paper.

"Let's print our suggestions," said Patience. "It'll make them more mysterious."

So they did this, and the folded slips of paper were put into one of Mr. Kane's hats, and given a good shake. Then Peter chose one, and read out:

" 'Go after gipsies and see if they have got King T'."

"Oh, you've chosen mine," cried Patience, "though I put Toby, not T——"

"It's mine," declared Susan, "but I said 'Follow' instead of 'Go after'——"

"And I didn't mention gipsies at all," said Gerry, "I just put 'Look for cat!' "

"The one Peter just read to you is mine," said Rough. "I put T for short. Don't you see what's happened? We've *all* suggested looking for Toby. You did, didn't you, Tough?"

His twin nodded, and Peter flipped through the papers.

"Yes, everyone's written something like that—except Georgie. Yes, it's printed, but I'd know her fist anywhere. She says: 'Lads (on bicycles) to show the moor to Sue and Patience (on horses). Picnic meals packed by Mrs. Duncan and Georgie.' That's the lot, then, as—being the umpire—I didn't enter. I'll have to think about this," he said seriously.

"Oh, why?" cried Tough.

"Yes, Peter, *don't* 'Don't'," begged Susan. "You're not grown-up. You're not seventeen till next week. . . ."

"Have you ever tackled gipsies, Susan?" he countered good-humouredly. "I don't mean the harmless town variety, who go about selling flowers and clothes-pegs. I mean real ones—in a bad mood."

"No, I haven't," she answered. "Have you?"

"Cheek!" muttered Gerry, and even Georgie frowned at her rash friend. But Peter answered pleasantly that he had not.

"I don't think it would be a particularly funny job," he said. "That's why I'm hesitating. You see, it's not as if I could come with you——"

Susan coloured at this reminder that Peter could not yet get about like other people.

"I'm an ass," she said. "A born one. Ask Georgie—she knows."

"You're not," Peter said at once. "I think it's grand of you all to want to find Toby. I'm just trying to think of ways and means. The only thing I can think of is—to combine that suggestion with Georgie's. How would it be if you did go and see the gipsies—in a friendly sort of way—on horseback and on bicycles? Only you'd have to promise before you started that you'd keep together and not do anything silly. . . ."

"Oh, *Peter*," cried Georgie, her hazel eyes shining with excitement. "How could we manage it? Timbo and Candy for Sue and Patience, and the Lads have their own bicycles. Gerry could borrow Mother's—you could lower the saddle—and I'm sure Mrs. Duncan would let me have hers. And of course we wouldn't do anything stupid—we don't *want* to get the gipsies' backs up. If we took some money with us and let them tell our fortunes, we'd have time to look for Toby."

"And the Leadbetters' twenty pounds," said Susan, who could be very tenacious when she liked.

"We can hardly expect to see that, unless they've papered the caravan walls with it," said Gerry, with dreadful sarcasm. "But Toby's sure to come out of hiding the moment he hears Georgie's voice, so it's worth trying. You can count me in." She added crossly: "Though I don't see why we need go out like a carnival procession. Why not bus to Periton like reasonable human beings?"

"Because the gipsies aren't *in* Periton," Susan cried in exasperation. "They're on the moor—Patience and I saw them in the distance this afternoon——"

There had been no time to tell the others of this discovery. The Kanes, and even the superior Gerry, plied them with eager questions.

"If you saw them from Widgett's Tor, they were probably near Medlicott," Tough said thoughtfully. "That's a tiny village where they're having a gymkhana and show to-morrow, and the travelling circus as well. We saw it billed in Periton. Well, Georgie, it's a long shot—but if it's O.K. by Peter, what about trying? There's quite a decent track to Medlicott, and I think the bikes can just about manage it."

"And the horses can do it on their heads," Susan solemnly averred, "so that's settled—isn't it, Peter?"

He hesitated, and at that moment the telephone rang. He was nearest the door, so he answered the call, while the others listened anxiously, guessing that it was from Mrs. Kane.

"Oh, hallo, Mother. Is she? Good," they heard him say, and then: "I say, I must tell you—Aunt Kate couldn't come——"

"Oh, *why* do people have consciences?" Susan whispered fiercely, glaring at Peter's back.

"Oh, so you know that," Peter was saying. "Yes

—they're all right. No, Toby hasn't come back. The others were thinking of going over to Medlicott to-morrow—— Yes, all right, Mother. I will. Good-bye."

He came back smiling. "Great-Grannie's a bit better, and Mother's heard from Aunt Kate, and doesn't mind our being on our own. And she doesn't mind about Medlicott either. I'm to ring up again to-morrow night. Well, there's nothing to stop your going to-morrow. I only wish I could come too."

They all wished this, but Susan was the only one to offer a suggestion as to how he should spend his time.

"It's just as well that *one* of us should stay behind—to get supper, you know. Mrs. Duncan will go before we get back, and you'll have heaps to do in the kitchen. . . ."

Patience looked horrified, but Peter laughed.

"I'm a dab hand at sago pudding," he said cruelly, and Susan groaned.

"As you're so keen on food," Gerry said to her, "you may like to get up early and cut sandwiches. Or perhaps you'd better not."

Susan bit her lip. She could stand any amount of teasing as a rule, but Gerry's manner was one which a cherub could not fail to resent. Georgie reflected uneasily that these two would almost certainly have a first-class row before long.

"I'll cut the sandwiches," she said decidedly, "and Patience can dilute the lemon squash and fill all the bottles we can find, while Susan goes to borrow Timbo. Candy we can pick up as we pass. And, Gerry, could you go and borrow Mrs. Duncan's bike for me, and coax like mad?"

Gerry looked mollified by this request, as Georgie had hoped she would. Rough and Tough promised to alter the saddle of their mother's bicycle, and soon the plans for the morrow were practically complete.

"But there's one thing we mustn't forget," declared Susan, "and that's a basket to bring King Toby home in!"

Georgie had already thought of this, but it was cheering to find that Susan felt so sure that they would get him back.

They went to bed early, as they wanted to start on their quest betimes. Georgie borrowed her mother's alarm clock, and it really seemed as if it roused her before she had had five minutes' sleep. She jumped out of bed and dashed from room to room, thumping doors.

There followed a very busy hour, and then, after an unconventional but remarkably hefty breakfast, the adventurers set forth. Peter waved them good-bye, pretending that he didn't mind being left, but of course he did really. The spaniels crouched at his feet, their brown eyes pleading; but the journey was far too long for them, even if Rough and Tough had allowed them to follow bicycles.

"Keep your fingers crossed for us, Peter," were Georgie's parting words, "and when Mrs. Duncan comes, ask her to make a huge pie or something. We'll *all* be ravenous when we get home to-night."

It did not occur to any of them that the business of getting home might present some difficulties.

If Georgie had been less worried about King Toby, she would have revelled in the glorious air and sunshine of that perfect morning. As it was, she was able to see the beauty of the countryside, and laugh at the baby rabbits who bounded for shelter at the humans' approach. They called at the farm, and Susan went in to fetch Candy. Here the first snag occurred. Mrs. Leadbetter refused to let her have him.

"No, my dear, not with that cut on your arm barely healed. Why, it's only two days since your tumble—

yes, thank you, Jet's doing well and all, but that's neither here nor there."

"But I went out yesterday," argued Susan. "I went nearly to Widgett's Tor——"

"Yes, miss, but that's not like going to Medlicott-in-the-Moor. You look none too grand. Supposing that cut breaks open? No. I'm a mother myself, and I'd never let Connie ride all day with an arm like that."

It was at this point that Georgie spoke up.

"Mrs. Leadbetter, is Candy really a—a peaceful kind of cob? Does he buck when a novice is riding him? Is he liable to run away?"

"Now, Miss Kane, is it likely that we'd let your mum hire him for the young ladies if he was like that?" asked the farmer's wife, quite incensed. "He's a proper little gentleman, is Candy."

"Then I'll ride him," said Georgie, "and Susan can have my bike. If I keep close to Patience and Timbo, nothing much can happen. . . ."

There was a moment's silence. They all looked at her with respect.

"You can't do that, Georgie; you haven't ridden at all," said Susan. "I'm sorry I made such a fuss. Of course I won't come—I'll go home."

She found that now she had accepted her disappointment bravely, everyone was determined to help.

"I'm right sorry," said Mrs. Leadbetter, "but you don't want a bad arm, do you? Tell you what—Mr. Jones the vet is going over to Medlicott by road. He's taking his wife and little girl, but maybe there's room for you too." And she bustled into the house and telephoned, returning in triumph. "He's just starting, miss. He'll pick you up along the road."

They thanked her heartily, and set off. Jet whinnied quite contentedly when Susan spoke to him, which cheered her very much.

"What a piece of luck about the vet," she gloated. "Now I'll have a good look at the gymkhana before you people get to Medlicott at all. Shall I come and meet you by the gipsies' encampment, or will you come and fetch me?"

"Oh, we'll come to you," said the others, in one voice.

"We don't know where the gipsies are, but anyone will tell us the way to the gymkhana," Georgie added. "If you stay with Mr. and Mrs. Jones, nothing awful *can* happen. . . ."

"Huh!" said Gerry. "Anything can happen on a wild goose chase like this."

They stayed on the main road with Susan until Mr. Jones's little car hove in sight, and then the five travellers set off down the winding track across the moor, towards Widgett's Tor. Georgie, bringing up the rear on Mrs. Duncan's antique bicycle, reflected with an inward smile that Gerry hadn't been so far out when she had likened them to a carnival procession. Patience, riding Timbo and wearing Susan's jodhpurs and jacket, looked quite astonishingly picturesque, with her thick fair braids neatly doubled up, and the light of pure happiness on her face. Gerry, just behind her, was less romantically mounted on Mrs. Kane's bicycle, which was used for village shopping only, and had been disfigured by two enormous baskets, now crammed with provisions. The Lads cycles were of a very different type, with racing handlebars and slim, greyhound wheels; but the Lads themselves had come prepared for anything. Rough had a portable tent strapped to his back, and Tough had fishing rods. On the carrier of Mrs. Duncan's machine Georgie had strapped an old suitcase, with a number of holes punched in the lid. This was for the errant Toby.

Timbo was conscious of the freshness of the morn-

He wanted to break away.

ing air. He wanted to break away, but Patience would not let him until they came to the tor. Then she gave him his head, and he climbed half way up, as he had the day before.

"I can't see a sign of the gipsies now," she ex-exclaimed, in bitter disappointment.

"They've moved on, that's all," Rough called back to her. "I thought they would. They're in Medlicott now, I bet, all ready for the gymkhana. Come on, Patience—now we'll *really* get cracking. It's a decent path, and downhill now for several miles, so—here goes. . . ."

He pedalled away, closely followed by his twin. Patience got Timbo safely down from the tor, and cantered after them. Georgie looked at her cousin, expecting to hear another grumble, but by this time Gerry had caught the excitement of the chase.

"Race you," she laughed, and rattled along the uneven track with an abandon that made Georgie blink.

CHAPTER FIVE

PATIENCE IS MYSTERIOUS

BEFORE they had gone very far, the track became more difficult, and for two or three miles ran steadily uphill. This did not affect Patience, but the four cyclists had to push their machines, as the soft grey sand was apt to clog the wheels. The day was growing warmer, and every now and then someone would pause to discard some garment.

"Susan's had the best of it," Gerry said at last, when they reached the brow of a hill, and saw nothing but rolling moor ahead of them. "How much farther have we got to go?"

"Not much," said Tough, but the mention of Susan

had brought a welcome idea to his mind. He looked at Georgie, who nodded.

"Yes, why not? We'll have a rest and something to eat before we go another step."

"Look here," said Patience. "I'm not hungry—why shouldn't I ride on to the next hill, and then come back and report? I fell sure I'll be able to see Medlicott from there, and also there's a stream where Timbo could get a drink."

"Good idea," said Georgie. "Have a sandwich first, though. I've some carrots for Timbo."

She fed the pony quite as a matter of course, while her brothers looked on.

"Gosh, Georgie, do you remember how you fed Mr. Primrose's horse with a toasting fork?" said Tough, but subsided when his brother nudged him. Georgie laughed.

"I did," she admitted gaily, "but Firefly wasn't a nice, cosy, fobsy little chap like Timbo. There, that's the last carrot. See you later, Patience."

It was good to sit on the springy turf and eat the rather crumbly sandwiches which she herself had cut at dawn. The lemon squash was very refreshing, and the weary cyclists made the most of their picnic. They prudently rationed themselves, however, for although they had brought money with them, it was impossible to say whether they would be able to buy any food. They had just finished packing up when Patience came back, her cheeks unwontedly flushed.

"Yes, we're quite near Medlicott, I think," she reported. "I could see roofs in the distance, and there's a road about half a mile away. I met some other riders—going to the gymkhana, I suppose—and they were very rude."

"Rude, Patience? What did they say?" demanded Tough.

"It was Timbo they were rude to—not me," Patience said indignantly. "They were two boys and two girls about our age or a bit older, and they called out, "Are you going in for the Under Eleven race, or what? Where *did* you find that quadruped?" And then one of the girls laughed and said, 'Don't look so peeved. I like the way you've done your hair.' "

"Did they think they knew you?" asked Georgie.

"I don't see how they could have. No, they were just naturally rude," said the ruffled Patience, as she patted Timbo's neck. "Quadruped, indeed. . . ."

"Well, if we're ready, we might as well go on," said Rough, "as this show will probably start before lunch. I expect Susan's there already. No sign of the gipsies, I gather?"

Patience shook her head. "I didn't go far enough. I turned back after those creatures had insulted Timbo."

"You do make a fuss about nothing," said Gerry. "You ought to come to St. Monica's—we'd knock some sense into you then."

But Patience, with her odd little air of dignity, pretended not to hear, and soon the procession had moved on again.

Georgie had been through Medlicott several times in the car, but she had never had the chance to explore it. Now she saw that it was a very pretty little place, with white-washed cob cottages, heavily thatched in the Devonshire tradition, and a crystal stream running by the side of the main road. There was no high street, but some shops were scattered here and there round a beautiful old green, with a duckpond in the middle. Some tethered goats were grazing here, staring disapprovingly at the two gipsy caravans which had drawn up by the side of the green. A large finger-post had been put up nearby, saying "To Horse Show & Gymkhana."

"It's pointing to that big field," Patience began, "and I can see Sue over there——" She broke off when she saw that Georgie was not listening, but had her eyes fixed on the caravans.

"Georgie, don't——" began Tough; but it was too late. She was running across the green, jingling two half-crowns in her hand. That noise was evidently sweet music to the occupants of those caravans, for as she approached, at least twenty brown faces seemed to appear in the narrow doorways and at the tiny curtained windows.

"*What* a pretty little lady!" exclaimed a fulsome gipsy with enormous earrings and such a terrific squint that one didn't know which eye to talk to. "Shall I tell 'ee the future, love?"

"Er—no, thanks," said the blushing Georgie. "I just wanted to know if you'd any cats for sale?"

"That we have, lady," said a gipsy boy, in a hearty tone, and Georgie's hopes began to rise. But, alas, they were dashed to the ground when, a moment later, he held up a thin and miserable tabby with a bleeding paw.

"Haven't you a ginger one?" she asked faintly.

"No," said the squinting gipsy, "you can't beat the tabbies for mice. Beautiful cat, this one—you wait till she gets her summer coat. We didn't want to part with 'er, reelly——"

"That's all right, then," said Georgie. "I want a ginger one, you see——"

She started in dismay, for the boy, with an angry mutter, had apparently flung the poor cat away from him. Georgie heard a thud and then a hopeless miaou.

"Oh, you've hurt it," she said sharply, but the faces had all disappeared by now, and the only answer was a laugh.

Georgie waited a second, and then stepped forward.

"How much is that tabby?" she demanded.

"Five shillings to you, little lady," wheedled the elder gipsy, reappearing as if by magic; and Georgie knew that, notwithstanding her squint, she must have seen those two half-crowns. However, one could not leave the unfortunate tabby cat with these people, and this was no time to haggle. She handed over the money and received a struggling shape which promptly scratched her neck and bit her finger.

"*Well,*" said Gerry, surveying the discomfited Georgie as she brought back her purchase. "Sometimes I think you're crazy, and other times I *know* you are. . . . D'you mean to say you paid for it? Why, Mr. Jones will have to put it to sleep."

"I don't know," said Patience, dismounting to have a look at the tabby, which had grown calmer now. "That's a wound on its paw—not a disease. Let's open one of the meat sandwiches, and put it with the cat into the suitcase."

They were doing this when a car passed them, and stopped. A tall, handsome woman in tweeds got out and came towards them, and they saw that she wore a medal with the word JUDGE on it, pinned to her coat.

"What's happened?" she said to Patience. "Poor cat—did you kick it, or what? Oh, the gipsies had it, had they? Well, it's quite healthy, I should say. I suppose it will join the rest of the menagerie?" She smiled at them all, and patted Patience's shoulder. "Good luck, my dear. By the way, I like your hair like that."

And she hurried back to the car.

"She thinks you're going in for the gymkhana," Georgie observed, with furrowed brows, "but why all these remarks about your hair? *This* one didn't mean to be rude, anyway. There, Stripo's safely fastened up now, so we'd better go to Susan."

"Patience," said Tough, "why don't you?"

"Why don't I what?" asked the girl, as she led Timbo across the road in the direction indicated by the finger-post.

"Go in for the Gymkhana now you're here."

"Tough, I couldn't. With all these strangers? Besides, one has to enter beforehand. I shouldn't like to," Patience said, looking round rather nervously. "I—I don't want these people to stare at me."

"It isn't you they're staring at," Gerry told her flatly. "It's all of us, and I can't say I'm surprised. I only *hope* we shan't meet anyone from St. Monica's."

However, Susan had caught sight of them by this time, and came running towards them, and they straightway forgot their embarrassment at their own strange appearance in their pleasure at seeing her again.

"Mr. and Mrs. Jones were sweet," Susan told them enthusiastically, "especially as it was a fearful squash, and Mrs. Jones had to have little Betty on her lap. I showed her my cut, and she thinks it's healing beautifully, so I *could* have ridden over perfectly well. Still, I'm to go back with them at seven o'clock. You'll have to leave before then, won't you?"

"I should think so," said Rough. "We don't want to lose our way and have to camp on the moor. Have you seen any gipsies in the field? There are some in the village, but they don't seem to have got Toby."

"I've been looking, but I haven't seen any," Susan answered, "though we did pass some on the way over just a few hundred yards from the road, by a pond. I wanted to go and ask, but Mr. Jones said there wasn't time. But the travelling circus is here all right, only it isn't open yet."

"Well, we'd better go in," Georgie decided, as they neared the entrance. The boys had already placed the bicycles in an improvised park, and Patience saw no reason why she should not bring Timbo in as a spectator. But the man who was taking the admission money shook his head at her.

"Competitors other entrance," he said. "Can't you see the notice?"

"Yes, but——" Patience began, when a tall, lanky girl of sixteen or so slapped her on the shoulder.

"Come on—you're blocking up the gangway," she said breezily, and gave Timbo a searching stare. "What do you call your quadruped, anyway?"

Patience twisted away from her, and turned a flushed face to Georgie.

"She's one of those people who spoke to me on the road," she said in a low voice. "She seems to want to tack on to us, but I'll give her the slip. Timbo's tired—I'm going to see if they'll stable him at the inn."

Georgie nodded rather abstractedly, for Susan had just dashed up to report that she could hear miaous issuing from the closed caravans of the travelling circus. As soon as Patience had gone, therefore, leading the bewildered Timbo, she and Tough approached the circus, only to be shown a fierce-looking parrot, who could imitate cats and dogs "better than life," as his proud owner said.

"Oh, well," said Georgie, who was becoming used to disappointments, "I think we'd better go and find seats now. That man with the microphone's giving out that Class One's just going to start. Quick, get a programme, someone."

As it was still so early, there was plenty of room in the field, although spectators and performers were arriving all the time. It was a lovely day for a gymkhana—warm and bright without being dazzling, and except for her grief about King Toby, Georgie would have felt very happy as she settled down in the front row of the roped-off seats. Susan was beside her, and a place was kept for Patience on Georgie's other side.

It was a very large field, and had been well arranged. There were two rings, one in which the events were taking place, and the other reserved for showing. The first one was naturally the more interesting, though Susan kept on making excursions to Ring Two, for Mr. Jones was one of the judges here, and she had promised to help him if he needed her. He did not, of course—there were dozens of horsey friends waiting to do this—but Susan kept her word.

The first events were confined to children and their ponies, and Georgie was impressed at the skill and pluck shown by these small creatures. The boys were fascinated too, and even Gerry forgot to be critical as she watched the Best Kept Ponies, Best Rider under Eleven, and Juvenile Jumping. They all clapped loudly when a podgy six-year-old whose pony refused a jump patted it and whispered encouragement before trying again, and they all frowned on the child who lost her temper and was sent off for hitting her mount.

It was only when they had time to breathe again that Georgie and Susan looked at each other, and asked "Where's Patience?"

There was a blank little silence, and then the twins said they would go and look for her.

"She was going to stable Timbo at the inn. One of us ought to have gone with her," said Rough. "I expect the stables were full, and she's taken him somewhere else. We'd better go in different directions, Tough."

"Oh, no, stick together, *please*," begged Georgie, "or one of you will get lost next. . . ."

"We won't. We'll come back here in twenty minutes," the boys promised, and wriggled their way out of the now crowded rows of chairs.

They did separate, as soon as they reached the gates, and Rough was the first to return. His usually cheerful face looked distinctly cross, and he only nodded in response to Georgie's anxious question.

"Isn't Paish coming?" cried Susan, craning forward.

"No," said Rough. "She said she'd rather not."

Mr. Jones was one of the judges.

"*What?*" gasped all three girls together, and someone from behind said with grim politeness: "*Would* you mind keeping still for the next sixty seconds? My son is in this race."

Abashed, they waited till the race was over, and then questioned Rough again.

"Where *is* she? And why doesn't she want to sit with us?" Georgie demanded wrathfully.

"She was outside the gates, talking to some people. I said 'Hallo, Patience', and she said 'Hallo'. Then I told her we'd got a seat for her and wouldn't she come, and she said no, thanks, she'd rather not—and looked at me as if I were an insect. So I told her to get on with it," he said, in pardonable annoyance.

"But it isn't like her. She—oh, here's Tough," said Georgie, signalling to the other twin.

"*Would* you mind——" murmured the voice from behind. "My nephew is jumping now. . . ."

Tough sat down, with a broad grin.

"I found Paish all right," he told the others. "She'd just stabled Timbo, and said someone was going to lend her a mount and put her in for the last-minute entrants' race, which will be later on. She seemed awfully surprised."

Georgie stared. "Did she tell you that she didn't want to sit with us?"

"What on earth do you mean? She'll join us after she's ridden," said Tough, wide-eyed. "I stopped in the car park, by the way, and had a look at the cat. He's fast asleep inside the suitcase, so that's all right. Patience said that the gipsies you bought him from had called out to her and wanted her to buy a charm."

"And did she?" asked Susan.

"No, because she'd no money with her. But I lent her some, and she was rather bucked, because she said she wanted to get it for Mother," Tough explained, and noticed for the first time the scowl on his brother's face.

"Patience wasn't like that with me," was all Rough said. "I must have put my foot in it somehow. . . ."

"*Would* you mind?" murmured the voice again. "My little niece—ah, thank you; now I can see her."

As Georgie was wondering how many more relations her neighbour could possibly have, Susan nipped her arm.

"*Look,*" she breathed.

CHAPTER SIX

MORE SURPRISES

THE event now about to begin was a Pair Trotting Race, and the three Kanes, Gerry, and Susan sat absolutely spellbound as Patience rode into the ring, one of a merry group of boys and girls of her own age and younger, for this race was for people under fourteen.

"But—you have to *practise* for this sort of thing," gasped Susan, the first to find words, "because you have a partner, you see, and you have to hold hands as you go. And Paish is the very last person to do anything like that on the spur of the moment—— Why, Georgie, you know she'd never even ridden astride in public till she came to Devon."

"She's a dark horse," said Gerry. "I knew it from the first. That's the way with these meek, butter-won't-melt people. Just look at her now."

"We—*are* looking," said Georgie, and rubbed her eyes. Patience, the shy, the retiring, was going to lead the field. Her partner was a girl of about the same age, mounted on a piebald pony. Patience's pony was white, but matched the other exactly in regard to size and what Tough called "make", and Patience and the other girl were laughing together like old friends.

"Line up——" shouted the blurred voice down the microphone, as the judges tried to get the field in order. "I want you to line up better than that. First couple a little forward, Miss Patience——" The voice died away to a mumble.

"Did you catch her partner's name?" Susan asked Georgie.

"No, I can't hear what this man says. He didn't even get Patience's name very clearly. Oh, now I hear him

—he's speaking better. He's asking for stewards," said Georgie. "What *does* he mean?"

"Why, people to help," explained Susan. "It's often done. Stewards are people who aren't competing, but who are used to horses. They stand where they're told in the ring, and then they can help if the horses have to be held or anything. I say, he's pointing in this direction. Listen, he says he wants some stewards down this end. I believe I'll go."

She scrambled under the rope as she spoke, and Gerry muttered something about showing off.

"She's not," Georgie said hotly. "She's going to help—and what's more, *so am I*."

And she followed Susan before she had time to regret her hasty decision. After all, she was used to horses even if she couldn't ride yet. Susan gave her an approving grin.

"Nothing happens as a rule, but it gives the riders confidence to know we're here," she said grandly.

Nothing untoward did happen in that race, which Patience and her partner won easily. Their ponies might have been brothers, by their similarity of action, and the two girls managed to hold hands all the time. A number of the others failed to do this, and became disqualified. The riders had to go twice round the field. Patience must have seen Georgie and Susan, but she took no notice of them whatsoever.

The next race was a very amusing one for the small children. It was a musical one, a variation of the famous nursery game, and the competitors enjoyed it to the full. Only one child missed her footing when she tried to remount, and Georgie, who was nearest her, went forward quietly and grasped the pony's bridle. The little girl mounted successfully this time, and smiled her thanks.

"Will the stewards please stay where they are for

Patience and her partner won easily.

the next race?" came the voice from the microphone, and added some more sentences which Georgie did not catch. Susan came over to her.

"Did you hear what he said? Well, it's jumping now —over twelve and under twenty-one, so there'll be some big horses. Want to go back to the others, Georgie?"

Georgie *did* want to, for a few seconds, because one of the brushwood jumps was being erected quite near where she was standing; but she thought of Rough and Tough, who wouldn't like to see her admit defeat, and for some reason she thought of the Grange, and her friends there. She didn't want to let them down.

"Oh, I'll stay," she said lightly, and then saw to her relief that her brothers were coming to join her.

"We're going to be stewards too," said Rough. "A chap behind me was saying that you can't have too many when it's jumping. Sure you want to stay?"

She saw that they had come to give her a chance to retire.

"Might as well," she said briefly. "As you say, the more the merrier—— Oh, look, they're coming in by the Competitiors' entrance. Golly—Sue, do you see what I see? Patience is in this too!"

"But—this is jumping. *Stiff* jumping at that. Her last-minute entrants' race isn't till much later. Oh, I don't understand this a bit," groaned Susan, as she took up her position.

The jumping began. Georgie didn't like it at all, because the ground seemed to shake and quiver as the huge black horse ridden by the first competitor came thundering by. He tossed his mane and rolled his eyes as he snorted like a war-horse in an old tale of jousts and tourneys; and the young man who rode him looked stern and pale—just like Pluto, thought poor Georgie, when he came to seize Proserpina. She stood her ground, however, and then saw that the black horse, for all his grand display, had funked an easy jump. She saw the young man bite his lip while he made a dramatic gesture and withdrew to try again, and realized that horse and rider were both nervous, and only pretending to be fierce. She wished she could speak to the black horse and tell him not to worry, and give him a bit of apple, perhaps, to cheer him up. But there was no time for anything like that. Her sympathy, however, must have shown in her very expressive face, for the rider glanced at her as he passed, gave a faint, boyish grin, and muttered a quick, "Keep your wool on, old chap," to the horse. This time they cleared the brushwood beautifully, and galloped off to the next jump, which had been built up to look like part of a roof, with a chimney at one side.

On the whole, the standard of jumping was very high. As usual with these country gymkhanas, people had come from all over the place, while to judge by the number of spectators, Medlicott and its surrounding hamlets had decided to have a mass holiday.

Patience came towards the end. She was not riding the white pony now, but had a beautiful bay of at least fifteen hands. She was certainly the best-looking girl on the field, with the sun glinting on her fair braids, still doubled up under her bowler.

"Where did she get *that* from?" Susan asked Georgie, just before Patience broke into a gallop. "I hadn't a hat, so she's borrowed it from someone else, and—I believe she's borrowed another jacket too. You have a look when she comes."

But Georgie did not trouble to look at Patience's clothes. It was the girl herself who engaged her attention. She had not known that Patience could ride like this—with an effortless arrogance which made the spectators gasp. What a lovely horse that bay was!

Who could have lent him to a complete stranger?

Patience did not look at them, of course. She had no chance to do that. They could see that every nerve was taut as she and the bay approached the brushwood jump, which they cleared with astonishing grace. Spontaneous clapping came from all over the field. Amongst the audience Georgie saw the tall, handsome woman who had spoken to them earlier in the day, and asked Patience if she had accidentally kicked the tabby cat. She had judged the last event, but was evidently resting now, and clapping harder than anyone.

Now came the roof jump. The bay didn't like it. He stopped short and refused point-blank, and Georgie sympathized with him. After all—why a roof? He was a horse, not one of Father Christmas's reindeer. . . .

Patience did not lose her head, nor show the slightest sign of discomfiture. She simply tried again. This time the horse cleared the jump, but she came forward too much and somehow pitched over his head. She got up at once—long before any of the stewards could reach her—and she might have been all right if she had not stumbled again, and this time knocked her head against the wooden chimney.

A man steward caught the bay, and Georgie was the first to reach the girl, who was struggling to her feet.

"Careful, Patience. Sit still for a bit," Georgie suggested, seeing how white she had become. But Patience moved her shoulders impatiently and muttered, "Don't *fuss*. . . ."

And then Georgie was thrust back as some ambulance men and other grown-up people, amongst them the tall woman with "Judge" on her coat, came up to see what had happened to Patience.

She seemed to be unharmed. At least, she said she was, and went off quite cheerfully with the grim young man who had ridden the black horse, in the direction of the refreshment tent. Georgie and Susan looked at each other.

"Well, she doesn't want us any more, that's obvious," Georgie remarked, trying not to sound as hurt as she felt. "But I shall never understand how Patience, of all people, could change like that."

"There are lots of things *I* don't understand," Susan said darkly. "I don't know much about gymkhanas—I've only been in for one, when I was quite small, but I'm sure Mummy entered me beforehand. I'm sure people don't just walk in. Let's have a look at the programme when we go back to Gerry."

It was nearly lunch time now, and an interval followed, during which the Lads went out to the bicycles and returned with the rest of the provender and the news that the tabby was still asleep. They were followed by Mr. Jones, the vet from Driscoe, who had come from the other ring to see Susan.

"The wife sent these," he said to Georgie, handing her a bag of buns. "She meant them for our tea, but we shan't be stopping now. I'm very sorry, Miss Walker, but plans have changed, and I can't help myself. Some of the animals I was to help judge haven't turned up and won't till tomorrow, and as I've had an urgent call from one of the farms near home, I reckon I'll have to get back. I'm awfully sorry to cut your day short like this——"

"Why, it can't be helped," said Susan, gulping back her disappointment. "It was jolly decent of you to bring me. Are you going back now?"

"Soon as possible. Say, in quarter of an hour. That'll give you time to get some lunch."

He strode away to find his car, and Rough and Tough came back from the refreshment tent carrying glasses of lemonade, the family supply having given out by this time.

"No, there was no sign of her," they said, when asked if they had seen Patience, and Rough added something to the effect that he wouldn't lose any sleep if he never saw her again.

"Let's go over there, under those trees, to have our lunch," said Gerry. "It's too hot here. No, I'm sorry, I haven't got the programme—that being who kept on saying 'Would you mind' borrowed it, and didn't give it back. Still, we shan't need it any more, shall we?"

"Well, you're staying a bit longer, aren't you?" asked Susan, but in a half-hearted tone. Since the curious behaviour of Patience, the gymkhana had lost much of its charm.

"Yes, but we'll go to the circus," said Rough, jingling his money nonchalantly to show that he would pay for this. They had reached the trees by this time, and he flung himself down on the cool grass—to start up again with a gasp, as he found that he had nearly landed on top of someone else.

"Gosh—it's Patience. She looks awful, too. Georgie, quick——" he cried.

Patience, who had been lying full length in the long grass, now raised herself on one elbow and looked at them in a dazed manner. Georgie saw a big bruise on her forehead.

"So you did hurt yourself," she began, and to her horror Patience burst into tears.

"It's only a bump. Do leave me alone. I only want to be quiet——"

"Why, Patience," said Georgie, "we're not going to bother you——"

"Don't call me Patience. I hate it. Call me Pat, if you must call me anything—— Oh, my head does ache so. I want to go home. . . ."

She groped for a handkerchief. Tough found his, and thrust it into her hand, while a strange expression flitted across his face. But nobody noticed that, for Georgie and Susan were too busy wondering how this new, hysterical Patience would ever manage the long ride home. It was Gerry, oddly enough, who found the solution.

"Listen, Susan, you say your arm's all right—well, why can't you ride Timbo home, and let Patience go in the Joneses' car?"

"Oh, Gerry, you genius," said Georgie, and turned to Patience, who was sitting up and looking much better. "Did you hear that? You're going home by car."

"But—but——" Patience muttered something like "pony".

"Sue will take him. We've got it all worked out. Come on—can you get up? You'll feel tons better when you're home."

Patience nodded, and a ghost of a smile played round her pale lips.

"Thanks awfully for bothering. I feel such a fool. Don't let any of these people see. I mean—one doesn't *do* this kind of thing. . . ."

She let the boys help her to her feet. As it was lunch time, the field was practically deserted. A few parties were picnicking here and there, but they managed to get Patience to the car park without encountering any of the pitying stares which she evidently dreaded. She looked more like herself now, but her head was obviously aching badly, and she didn't want to talk.

Mr. and Mrs. Jones and their little girl Betty were all ready and waiting, and when Georgie had explained about the alteration of plans, they made room for Patience in the small car, and put a rolled-up mackintosh behind her head.

"Good-bye. Tell Peter we won't be long," called Georgie, as the car moved forward, and the last thing she saw of Patience was the utter bewilderment in her deep blue eyes.

"I hope she hasn't gone crackers or something," Rough remarked cheerfully.

"I hope it isn't concussion," said Georgie. "Perhaps we oughtn't to have sent her by car. I'm almost sure she ought to have been kept still. But what *could* we do? We don't know anyone in Medlicott, and Mrs. Duncan will be there when she gets home. She'll put her to bed. Oh, why did it have to happen?"

"I think she went crackers *before* that bang on the head," said Susan. "Pretending not to know us and all that tosh. . . . Any sandwiches left?"

They went to the travelling circus, but only to assure themselves that King Toby wasn't there. The performance did not begin until three o'clock, and Georgie and Gerry were for once united in a resolve to start on their return journey in good time.

They collected Timbo from the stables at the Red Dragon, and Susan mounted him and went clattering into the village street, followed by the four bicycles. The caravans were no longer on the Green. Medlicott seemed remarkably empty, most of its population being still at the gymkhana.

"Its been fun," said Susan, "all except not finding Toby, or the money, and Patience's being so queer. I'd like to know who lent her that wizard bay. . . . How far do we have to go before we stop for tea?"

They quelled her, and took the narrow moorland road leading away from the village. They were all a little tired by this time, and perhaps that was why they paid scant attention to their surroundings. Rough was leading the party, and it came as a shock to everyone when he suddenly halted and turned round, frowning.

"I don't recognize this hill, do you?" he said. "I believe we-ve lost our bearings somehow."

CHAPTER SEVEN

THE LIMBER ELF

WHEN Rough uttered those frightful words, the others came to a standstill and looked round in dismay. Susan, who had come to Medlicott by car, was naturally unable to recognize her present surroundings, which were far from the main road; but to Georgie, Gerry, and Tough the moorland country looked familiar enough. There was the uneven skyline, there were the tors, the bright little streams, and the distant glimpses of the far-away, which always made Georgie think of A. E. Housman's phrase "*the coloured counties*". They were beautifully coloured now, by the glowing sunshine of that April afternoon.

"How wonderful it is," she breathed, leaning on her handlebars as she gazed around her in delight.

"It won't seem quite so wonderful if we're benighted on the moor," snapped Gerry. "We've come *miles* since that last fork in the road. Why on earth didn't you notice sooner, Rough?"

"Why didn't you?" asked Susan, dismounting. "Don't they teach you observation at St. Monica's?"

A battle seemed imminent, and Georgie signalled to the Lads for help.

"We must decide what to do. The road did fork, as Gerry says, some way back. Do you think we'd better retrace——?"

"No need, thank goodness," Tough cut in. "Look over there, to the left. That's the road we came by—if you can call it a road. I remember that hump-backed bridge, don't you? That's our track all right, and all we've got to do is cut across the moor to join it."

"Elementary, my dear young friend," said Rough, evidently quoting one of the prosier masters at their school, for a friendly wrestling match immediately took place. The girls were amused, but not so Timbo, who apparently disliked this form of sport. He pulled away suddenly, and Susan, who had been holding the bridle very lightly, felt it jerk out of her hands.

He was not really frightened, and made no attempt at first to run away. But he kept out of reach, and when Georgie, feeling very daring, went after him, he began to trot. Suddenly he stood still, arching his neck and sniffing the air. Far away to the right of them—in the opposite direction from the road they wished to join a herd of Dartmoor ponies was grazing at the edge of a chain of high rocks. There were three baby foals amongst them—dear little spindly creatures who kept close to their mothers.

"Oh, Timbo, don't go to them," Georgie entreated, as she snatched a handful of grass and held it out to him. "You ought to know what'll happen if you do. . . ."

But Timbo decided to risk it, and went galloping off to join the moorland ponies. There was a kind of stampede, and the mothers guarded their babies, while the fathers, all flashing hooves and flying manes, went pounding to meet Timbo. He stopped and whinnied, and then turned tail.

"First stop Dockleford, by the look of things," said Susan, with the calmness of despair.

"Tough and I can take you in turn on the back of our bikes," said Rough, and then gave an exclamation. "What's that blood on your arm?"

The cut had broken out again, just as Mrs. Leadbetter had feared it might, and Georgie felt secretly alarmed as she bound it up afresh. Susan stoutly affirmed that she was all right, but it was obvious that she ought not to put any strain on her arm at present. She realized this herself.

"I suppose I can't ride a bike to-day. It doesn't matter—I'll walk. Let's get down to that road, and then you four go on, and I'll just keep on hoofing it. I can't get lost that way, and will get to Dockleford sooner or later."

"You do think we're a set of monsters," Georgie cut in. "There's a better way than that. Gerry and one

Suddenly he stood still.

of the Lads must go on—because Peter'll be in a flap if nobody turns up—and the other Lad and I will walk with you."

"That won't work either," said Tough.

"Why not?" asked the three girls together, but Rough understood what he meant.

"Just have a look behind you," he suggested, and they turned. A heavy mist, white and dense, was rolling slowly towards them.

"Wh-what *is* it?" quavered Susan.

"What do you think?" snapped Gerry. "It's a fog,

of course—a Dartmoor Special—and it may last for *days*."

"We must get down to the road right away," said Rough, in an agitated voice, "just in case it's one of those very thick ones. Timbo'll find his own way home. I say, this ground is bumpy—I hope your cat's all right, Georgie?"

The tabby was, in fact, trying to get out of the suitcase by this time, and his frightened miaous roused Gerry to a fresh outburst of indignation.

"To think that we've landed ourselves in this spot just because Georgie was such a baby about Toby," she snorted.

"Oh, save that for when we get home, Gerry," said Susan. "Look here, are we going the right way? I'm going *up*hill—not down. . . ."

They all found that they were doing the same thing, and there was a short, bitter silence, broken by Georgie.

"How wonderful it would be if one of us could say just *something* that the others wanted to hear. Like 'I can hear a bus coming', or 'There's a signpost'——"

"Or 'Isn't that a tea-shop just in front of us?' " moaned Susan. "Oh, well, if we keep on walking, we're sure to get somewhere——"

"Yes, but it's not as simple as that," said Rough. "We can get hopelessly lost. There are bogs here, and nasty holes in the rocks. Do you know what I think?"

"I think so too," Tough said solemnly, quite forgetting that the girls could not read his twin's mind as he could.

But in this case Georgie was able to hazard a guess.

"You mean we ought to find a sheltered place and camp here for the night? But—what about Peter and Patience?" she asked in alarm. "They'll think something's happened to us."

"And they'll be right," said Susan, so tragically that they all burst out laughing. Even Gerry's lips twitched unwillingly.

"It might be worse," she said grudgingly. "There might have been snow on the ground. . . ."

But Georgie was still thinking about Peter and the anxiety she knew he would feel, and she was glad that the mist was now so thick that no one could see the two large tears that were trickling down her cheeks.

"Nothing's gone right since King Toby disappeared," she said sadly. "Great-Grannie's illness, and Sue's hurting her arm, and Patience's turning so peculiar—and now *this*."

"I don't suppose we've finished yet," Susan told her cheeringly. "I've a sort of idea that your mother will be simply livid when she hears about to-day——"

"And we'll probably all get fever and die," capped Gerry. "I'm sure we're near a poison belt, or something. Can't anyone else smell a most ghastly——?"

"*Girls!*" Rough exploded. "This is the last time I'll take any girls exploring with me. Fever—after a few hours on Dartmoor. Smells—well—hum. Poof, there *is* something——"

There was. They had halted now, having come to a kind of chasm between two rocks, and as they were hampered by the bicycles they were pushing, they were at a loss how to proceed. As they stood hesitating a whiff of something very unpleasant drifted towards them through the fog.

"We're on the edge of a marshy bit, I suppose," said Tough, "and it's been disturbed. They do smell awful if they get stirred up. Let's go back the way we came."

"If we can," said Gerry, darkly.

It wasn't easy, especially as Georgie barked her shins on Gerry's bicycle, but they did reach a much nicer place, where the rocky floor felt firm and dry, and they were just deciding to camp here when they heard a faint, thin scream.

"Oh, what's that?" cried Susan. "It can't be a pony, and there aren't any other people for miles and miles. . . ."

Georgie's spine grew cold, but Rough asked Susan how she knew.

"There may be someone else in the same boat as we are. Hallo!" he called, and waited.

Now there was a frantic scream, and a child's voice called "Mam! Mam!"

"Let's prop the bikes against the rocks. Stay with them, Sue, and guide us back here, won't you?" Georgie said, as she strained her ears in the gloom. The cry was repeated, and the boys ran forward.

"Over here—to the left," they panted.

Georgie and Gerry, close on their heels, heard the sound of a splash, and knew that they must have come upon one of the treacherous little ponds which are so much deeper than they look. To judge by Rough's exclamation, it was evidently a quagmire, and Georgie felt rather sick as her feet sank into squelchy mud. Then came the child's cry once more, and this time it was close to Georgie's right ear.

"Coming," she called back, and struggled across the oozy ground which soon fell away from her, leaving her in water that was more than waist-deep. She was afraid of falling, for although Gerry and the boys were not far away, the fog made it impossible to see them, and the mud was so very slippery.

However, before she had time to call further encouragement to the victim, whoever it might be, her knee touched something heavy, and she felt desperate little hands seize her dripping skirt. She bent, and her fingers touched wet curls.

"Mam—Mam——" shrieked the terrified child.

"It's all right—we'll take you to her," Georgie gasped, with chattering teeth, and called out "Got him!" to the others. Then, slipping, slithering, and still afraid of being sucked into the bog, she managed to seize the little creature and drag it to safety.

Gerry and the twins were very soon with her, and the shouts of the faithful—and extremely worried—Susan brought them all back to the spot where they had sheltered before. By a queer coincidence the fog began to lift almost immediately, drifting up and down in long, slow spirals, and making the wet members of the party feel colder and wetter than ever.

Georgie was having difficulty in holding on to the child, who was an agile little thing of six or seven. It was a girl, they saw now, dressed in an outlandishly long frock—hopelessly bedraggled, of course, and so wet that the girls wanted to take it off. But the child—a little gipsy, by her looks—hung on to it with boh hands and screamed defiance at them.

"We *must* get her dry somehow," Georgie declared, "or she'll get a frightful chill. And we'll have to let her wear our clothes. Everything of mine is damp except this scarf, but she can have that. . . ."

"She may as well have this old cardigan I've got on," said Gerry. "It's due for the rag-bag anyway."

"She can have *anything* of mine," cried the impetuous Susan.

"For goodness sake be careful of your arm," begged Georgie, "and don't give her too much—or you'll catch a cold yourself. Your woolly, then—you've got your blazer. What's your name?" she asked the struggling child.

"Mam . . ." was the furious answer. "Ma-a-am. . . ."

"She sounds like a goat," said Rough, eyeing the

exhibit with interest. Whether the child understood or not, she kicked him sharply on the shins.

"She's a little fiend, but she's awfully pretty," said Georgie, looking at the small brown face, with its black eyes, red lips, and mass of damp dark curls. "'Mam' must be her mother. I wish we could find her."

"Maybe they've gone on and left her behind," suggested Gerry, but Georgie silenced her.

"They wouldn't. They think a lot of her—look at her little earrings, and the bracelet, and the embroidery on this frock. I know what we could do—Lads, what about a fire? Then the heartbroken parents will come rushing——"

"And you can ask them about Toby and the twenty pounds, said Susan, the only one to remember the original purpose of the expedition.

"A fire," said Rough. "Is that all? Just a fire—in the middle of Dartmoor, when everything's sopping wet after that mist, and nobody's got any matches——"

"I've got matches," Gerry said smugly, as she opened her shoulder bag. "I brought them in case you boys forgot. . . ."

Rough thanked her with admirable self-control. They found what was left of their food and tried to make the child eat when, with great difficulty, they had changed her clothes. The boys set alight to all the wrapping paper, which, being grease-proof, burnt very well. They put on twigs and heather too, but without success. Everything was too damp.

And night was coming on.

"Let's shout," said Susan; so they did. The little gipsy tried to wriggle away from Georgie, and refused to eat anything. At intervals she reiterated her dismal cry for "Mam."

"If you think the parents are really worrying," said Tough, "Rough and I might reconnoitre a bit——"

"No, please don't," Georgie implored him. "You'll get lost next, and we'll *never* find each other, but haunt the moor for hundreds of years, mopping and mowing, and scaring travellers out of their wits. . . . Let's all stay here."

"And hadn't we better finish up the crumbs?" asked Susan. "Goatalina doesn't want to eat, and it looks so untidy. . . ."

"All right. I'll give some to the tabby, and we can share the rest," said Georgie, and doled out the small amount of unappetizing food which had suddenly become so precious.

They offered a morsel to "Goatalina", who again refused, but whose spirits seemed to have undergone a change. She actually smiled, and broke into a little wordless chant of her own. Georgie had firm hold of her hand, fearing that she would run away, and suddenly the little child began to skip to and fro, a queer little figure in her borrowed clothes.

"She's crackers," said Gerry.

"No—I think she can hear something we can't," answered Georgie, loosing the little brown hand as an experiment. "She reminds me of that bit in *Christabel*——

A little child, a limber elf,
Singing, dancing to itself——"

Peter would have known at once what she meant, but none of her present companions had read Coleridge. They looked blank, and then their faces changed as they heard swift footsteps on the wet turf. A second later two tall gipsy men burst upon them, and the elder and fiercer of the pair snatched up the child, snarling something over his shoulder at the silent little group.

"Oo—wait," Georgie exclaimed, and picked up the sodden dress which their unwilling guest had been wearing. The other gipsy took it from her, with a menacing scowl.

"*Well,*" said Susan, the first to find words, "I do think you might say thank you. And—look here—we're lost. Can't you tell us the way back to the Dockleford Road? And—and have you seen a c-cat——?"

Her voice was quavering by this time, because the men looked so very angry. The elder was holding the child, petting her, and obviously looking for injuries. He paid no attention whatsoever to Susan's remarks, but the other did just glance at her.

"Road—mile away," he said, pointing across the misty expanse of the moor. Then he nodded to his fellow gipsy, and they went swiftly away, without another word.

"Gratitude," sniffed Gerry. "I wish I hadn't given that little wretch my old cardigan. . . ."

"Oh, she had to have something," said Tough, "because she was soaked through. But I wish you three hadn't given your clothes away, because it's going to be jolly cold out here presently. I was wondering—are you girls game to take a chance, and try to work our way to the road?"

"It's nearly dark," Georgie faltered, fearing fresh disasters; but then she remembered that Susan had no pullover, and Gerry no cardigan over her thin shirt. She herself did not miss her scarf so much, though she was sorry to have lost it. It was one which her mother had knitted, ready for her to take back to school next autumn.

"We'd better go," she said, "if Gerry and Sue can face it. Peter and Patience will be so frightfully worried till we turn up."

The others were of the same opinion, and so a few minutes later they wearily began to push their bicycles across the uneven surface of the darkening moor.

CHAPTER EIGHT

HOME AGAIN

THE gipsy man had told them the truth. They found the road easily enough, and although a long walk lay ahead of them, and they were already tired, cold, and hungry, they felt like shouting for joy. The mist had now cleared as if by magic, and they gazed entranced at the most wonderful sunset they had ever seen. Delicate clouds, like fairy castles built of alabaster inlaid with gold, were massed against the western horizon while the crimson sun sank slowly out of sight. The sky changed before their eyes; new colours came, and the castles faded from view. Now there was a range of mountains round a still green lake in which was reflected the evening star. Now there was a golden city with towers and minarets. . . .

"It ought to be fine to-morrow," said Gerry, to whom a sunset like that was no more than a convenient barometer.

"If it doesn't rain," agreed Susan, with owlish solemnity; and the cavalcade set off in earnest.

The boys had dynamos on their cycles, but the decrepit machines which Georgie and Gerry had borrowed were without lights, and Rough and Tough would not hear of going on ahead. Fortunately for them all, the moon rose early, and helped them on their way. Susan's steps lagged slightly, for she was feeling the effects of her fall, and the boys hoisted her on to Rough's bicycle, and took it in turn to push her. This was all right until the ground began to rise, and they had to abandon the attempt.

"Phew, we're climbing a mountain," said Rough, "or is it——? Can it be? It *is*—it's Widgett's Tor. . . ."

Georgie recognized it now, having passed it often enough in the car. They were still a good way from home, but at least they knew where they were. The relief she felt was heightened when, a few minutes later, they heard a whinny, and saw a large shape looming ahead of them.

"It's Timbo," screamed Susan. "The angel—the pet. Just wait till I get hold of you, you fiend—you wretch—you *mule*!"

But Timbo didn't mean to be caught. He kept his distance, but he was one of the party again, and his presence reassured them.

"Just think what a lot of people must be foaming at the mouth and wondering what's happened to us," said Susan, not without gratification. "Peter and Patience, of course, and Mrs. Duncan, who's worrying about her bike, and Tom Mayne who must think we've pinched Timbo. Heigh-ho," she added, stifling a yawn. "Has anyone else ever felt the urge to go to sleep out of doors?"

"Not in April," said Georgie, afraid that Susan meant to try the experiment. "Let's play something—what about 'I packed my bag'?"

It was strange to try this hilarious indoor game while trudging along a lonely moorland road at night, but it did make them forget their tired legs and the empty feeling inside which grew worse whenever they thought of supper. When the Bag game was exhausted, they made lists of those enchanting collective nouns like a "wisp" of snipe, a "gaggle" of geese, and a "pride" of lions. The Lads seemed to know them all, though Gerry challenged some of their efforts.

"I'm perfectly certain there isn't a snippet of snakes, or a moose of mice. We did them all for General Knowledge at St. Monica's, and I'd have remembered——"

"Well, let's see if you remember the word for cats," Tough said imperturbably.

"There isn't one," said Gerry, all the more positively because she wasn't sure.

"Haven't you ever heard of a catastrophe of cats?" asked Susan, in a tone of pitying surprise, and before Gerry could answer, one of the boys called out, "The main road. We're in Dockleford."

They could scarcely believe it. By this time it was so late that all the inhabitants were in bed, and Georgie was somehow surprised at this, feeling that there should have been a deputation awaiting them. She wondered hungrily if Peter and Patience had got a meal ready. Probably Mrs. Duncan would have stayed to help. . . .

A few more minutes, and they were at Wychwood. Timbo had trotted on ahead, and they supposed he had gone home; but it was impossible to find out at this hour. So they hoped for the best, and coo-eed softly to Peter as they opened the familiar gate, and dragged their weary frames to the front door. There was a light in the sitting-room, and they heard the sound of his rather slow steps in the hall. Then he opened the door, and the five wanderers tumbled into the house, Georgie clutching the comatose tabby cat.

"Oh, Peter, we're sorry—we couldn't help it," she began breathlessly. "We've had an *awful* time. How's Patience? Is her head still aching?"

"One thing at a time," said Peter. "I've got a fire going, so you'd better sit down and recover, while I get you some hot drinks. What's wrong with you, Susan? Your arm's bleeding again."

"I strained it, I suppose. Yes, it did bleed—that's why we're late. I couldn't cycle. If Paish hadn't taken that purler, I'd have come home in the car, and everything would have been all right," said Susan, sinking into an arm chair and looking alarmingly pale.

Timbo had trotted on ahead.

"Oh, she fell, did she?" asked Peter. "Mr. Jones only knew that her head was aching, and she wouldn't tell me anything at all." He hesitated, and looked at Georgie. "I'm afraid she's pretty bad," he said. "Don't get the wind up, but you'll have to know. She's—well, she's lost her memory."

"*Patience* has? Oh, Peter, no! Where is she?" cried Georgie, forgetting all about being tired and hungry.

"In bed, and Mrs. Duncan's with her. Half a minute, I'll bring in the grub, and then I'll tell you properly," he promised, and limped out to the kitchen.

"If you hunted all over the world, you wouldn't find another Peter Kane," Susan murmured gratefully.

"You'd have a job to find another Susan Walker, I should think," grinned Tough, but Rough was looking worried.

"Wonder what's up with Patience. I believe she lost her memory *before* she fell. Remember I told you all how queer she was to me?"

Peter now came in carrying a tray on which were six thick kitchen cups, six plates, and a loaf, some butter, and a piece of cheese. There was a bulging cake tin, for before his accident he had been on many such expeditions, and remembered the appetite he used to bring home. He went back for the teapot, and the others took off their shoes and settled down to one of the best meals of their lives. Georgie put down some milk for the new cat, who lapped hungrily and then curled up on Mr. Kane's special chair.

"No sign of Toby, of course?" asked Peter, and Georgie shook her head.

"*Or* of the twenty pounds," yawned Susan, exhausted but persistent. "But we had plenty of thrills, all the same. I shall never forget Patience jumping—will you, Georgie?"

"I shall never forget anything about this day. Oh,

Peter, this tea is grand. Look here, do tell us more about Patience," said Georgie, looking curiously at her brother's troubled face.

"Mrs. Duncan can tell you more than I can, I expect. Mr. Jones came to the door this afternoon and said he'd brought your friend home, and would I come out to the car as she was being rather difficult. Well, I went—not knowing whether it was Patience or Susan—and there she was, looking furious and telling Mrs. Jones to turn the car. I said, 'Hello, Patience, what's up?' or something, and she said— 'Let me go at once, whoever you are, or you'll be sorry'."

"She was like that to me at the gymkhana," said Rough. "The girls' mad. It sticks out a mile."

"She *isn't*," said Georgie and Susan together. "We know her, you see. She's one of the very best. . . ."

"She may suit the Grange," said Gerry, "but she wouldn't last five minutes at St. Monica's. Either she's crazy, or she's the rudest person in the world."

"I'm going to see," Georgie announced, springing to her feet. "She's in the little bedroom, I supose?"

"Yes, and that's another thing. *She didn't know her way about the house*. I'm sure she wasn't acting," said Peter.

Badly frightened now, Georgie raced upstairs and into the old playroom, where Mrs. Duncan sat by the reading lamp, nodding over some knitting. Patience lay in bed with closed eyes, in her old-fashioned white cotton nightdress. She was moving restlessly, and muttering something. Georgie bent to listen.

"Mother, I'm lost—I've been stolen—I've been taken away, just as you said I might be. Isn't Jacko jumping well? Look, Rollo. Oh, Rollo, be careful—you give Tommy Tucker his head far too much. . . . I do feel funny. Mother, Mother, I want to go home. . . ."

Patience was saying these words—Patience, who had said only two days ago that she didn't remember her mother at all. The skin at the back of Georgie's neck prickled as it did sometimes when she listened to ghost stories.

"P-Patience——" she faltered, and the blue eyes flew open at once.

"Oh, it's you again," said this unfamiliar Patience. "Look here, whatever your game is, do for heaven's sake let me ring my mother. If it's money you want——"

"Money—oh, Patience, how can you?" choked Georgie, and Mrs. Duncan woke up and began to scold her.

"So you've come back, have you, and high time too," she said, all in one breath. "Real hard on Master Peter, it's been. Now don't you go upsetting poor Miss Patience, miss, who's gone out of her mind, poor lamb, and dear knows when she'll come to herself again——"

"I AM myself," said a furious voice from the bed, and then Patience groaned and put her hand to her head.

"There," said Mrs. Duncan, wringing out a compress in a basin of cold water. "Better go, Miss Georgie, and leave her to me."

"I want to go home," moaned Patience.

"All right, you can," said Georgie, "as soon as you're better. We won't keep you by force. I'll write to your guardian, shall I?"

But Patience's lovely blue eyes were blank.

"Guardian?" she echoed uncomprehendingly, and Georgie gave it up.

Susan had already gone to bed, and Rough and Tough had gone out with torches to see if Timbo had returned to his field. He had, so apart from the mystery of Patience, the day's adventures had been less disastrous than the travellers had feared. Georgie, Gerry, and Peter washed up together, and discussed the position. Peter told the girls that he had sent for Dr. Warnford, who had called in that evening and pronounced that Patience was suffering from concussion.

"He doesn't want her to be moved. He thinks she's better here than she would be in hospital, and Mrs. Duncan's staying with her to-night, and Mother will be home to-morrow."

"Mother will? Did she ring up, then? Oh, is Great-Grannie dead?" cried Georgie.

"No. Better. Tons better. Mother 'phoned before Patience was brought back," Peter said, "and it seems there was a misunderstanding yesterday. Aunt Kate went to a call-box and rang up Pencarne, to ask how Great-Grannie was, and spoke to Mother. She said she hadn't been able to come to us because of the workmen in her house, but Mother quite understood that she'd come to-day. Then, I suppose, she began to wonder, and rang me up to ask if Aunt Kate was here. She said she didn't mind our being on our own for one night, but she couldn't let such a state of affairs go on, so she's coming back to-morrow morning. That is, to-day," he grinned, looking at the clock. "You'd better get some sleep, you two, or you'll look like a couple of hags."

The hags went upstairs, yawning, so weary that they could scarcely undress. Gerry fell asleep the moment she lay down, but Georgie's nerves had undergone a great deal of strain during the last few hours, and, tired though she was, she could not relax. She lay quite still, but her eyes were wide open in the darkness, and a thousand scattered thoughts chased round and round her brain.

It was only the merest rustle that made her sit up, and a gasp broke from her when she saw a slim figure in riding kit, with long fair hair floating loose about its shoulders, struggling desperately with the window fastening. Georgie jumped out of bed and seized Patience by the arm, just as the other girl was clambering over the sill.

"Gerry—wake up. Help me," she cried hoarsely. "Mrs. Duncan——"

"Let me *go*," said Patience. She writhed like an eel in Georgie's grasp, and a second later she was free. She bounded to the bedroom door and out on to the landing. A loud crash proclaimed the fact that she had missed her footing in the dark and fallen down the stairs.

"What on earth——?"

"What's happened?"

The three boys had heard the commotion and come out of their rooms. Peter switched on the light.

"It's Patience," Georgie said faintly, and leaned over the banisters, expecting to see a recumbent figure. But there was no one to be seen.

"We'll have to find her," said Rough. "She might do anything, in the mood she's in now. You girls go back to bed—this is a job for us. But," he added, between his teeth, "when we do catch Miss Patience Best, we'll make her pay for this. . . ."

In a few seconds the twins had donned shorts and sweaters, and had rushed downstairs to begin their hunt. Mrs. Duncan stood on the landing with the girls, saying at intervals that she would never forgive herself for dropping off to sleep and letting her charge escape.

"There's not been a morsel of luck in this house since King Toby went," she wailed, "and—hark, Miss Georgie, one of the boys is calling you."

Rough's voice, raised in an exultant bird-call, was ringing through the house.

"We've got her, Georgie. Found her by the garden gate——"

Georgie, galloping down the stairs, saw her brothers standing triumphantly with a surprised-looking Patience between them.

"Patience—come back to bed," she said coaxingly. "You'll feel much better in the morning."

"And don't try any more tricks," growled Rough.

"*Tricks?*" echoed Patience. She tried to shake her arms free. "I don't know why you two are holding me like this—as if I were going to run away. And, Georgie, what do you mean—'come back to bed'? You—you're so queer. Haven't you missed me at all?"

CHAPTER NINE

SOMETHING FOUND

BEFORE Georgie could answer, Mrs. Duncan came forward and took charge of the situation. She was a strongly-built countrywoman, and it was nothing to her to pick up the thirteen-year-old Patience and carry her upstairs as if she were a baby.

"Leave her to me," she told the others, as she went.

"But—Georgie! Rough—Mrs. Duncan—what's the matter?" gasped Patience, as she was borne away.

"She's certainly got her memory back," Georgie said uncertainly. "She does know who we are. Oh, *how* I wish Mother were here."

"Well, standing down here in a roaring draught won't bring her any sooner," Gerry pointed out, and led the way upstairs.

This time Georgie did manage to fall asleep, but she woke up very early, and tiptoed across the room to the door of the old playroom where Patience was sleeping.

Mrs. Duncan opened the door in response to her cautious tap.

"Sleeping like a lamb," she said. "Quite changed, she is—just her gentle, sweet self again, after I carried her upstairs. She wanted to tell me a lot of nonsense, but I told her to wait. 'Wait till morning', I said, 'and Mrs. Kane will be back then'. So she just sighs and drops off. I think I'd better slip home now, Miss Georgie, because my husband can't go to work till I get back, because of leaving young Lily. I'll be here at my usual time. Poor Miss Patience will sleep for hours, by the look of her."

Georgie was of the same opinion. Patience looked absolutely exhausted. As a precaution, however, she removed the clothes which were lying on the chair by the bed, and carried them into her own room, where she put them in a drawer. Then Gerry stirred, and the cousins dressed silently, both determined not to disturb the mysterious guest.

Georgie went down in her bedroom slippers, so that she could come up from time to time to see Patience without making a noise. Susan and Gerry, in a state of armed neutrality, cooked the breakfast between them.

The morning papers arrived just as Susan was serving porridge which everyone was much too polite to call lumpy. Georgie picked up the *Driscoe and District Herald*, which appeared every Saturday, to see if her advertisement for the return of King Toby had been squeezed into that week's issue. Her eye, however, was caught by a large headline on the first page.

MEDLICOTT GYMKHANA: SENSATION

The gravest anxiety is felt by all those who——

"Here's Mother," yelled Tough. "I can hear the car."

With one accord, they abandoned their porridge and rushed into the garden. Yes, there was the new car turning into the garage gates, and Mrs. Kane, a little pale and tired, but smiling all the same, was looking out for them.

"My dears," she said, and, jumping out of the car, contrived to hug them all at once—Susan included. "Great-Grannie's so much better that I think she'll be able to stay with us a little longer. She sends her love. Yes, I'm all right," she said, in answer to Peter's question, "but I'd like to know what's been happening while I've been in Pencarne, and why Patience has been trying to run away——"

"Patience—running away? But—we caught her," said Georgie, staring at her mother whose smile had vanished now. "That was in the night, though I can't think how you knew. But——"

She broke off and nearly choked. Patience, who had been lying at the back of the car, now sat up with a jerk and looked her full in the face.

"Auntie, she's gone crazy," Gerry exclaimed. "We've had a fearful time——"

"But Patience seems to think *she's* had a fearful time," said Mrs. Kane, "and I want to know about it. I met her quite a long way down the moorland road, trying to run. I stopped and asked her where she was going, and she said—— 'I want to go home, but I don't really mind *where* I go, as long as it's not back to that awful house'. So I said nothing, but took her into the car, and she fell asleep."

"How was I to know that you belonged to them?" Patience burst out, while her glance, half angry and half frightened, flashed from Mrs. Kane to the bewildered family. "I thought—I thought——" She ducked her head and tried to get out of the car.

"No, you don't," said Susan, in trenchant tones.

"You've jolly well got to explain why you've got your knife into us like this. Mrs. Kane will think we've been cruel to you, and it isn't fair. Lost memory or not, *what have we done?*"

Patience brushed her hand across her eyes, and stood her ground.

"You've kidnapped me," she said quietly, "and you can't pretend you don't know it. You——" she paused, and looked inquiringly at Georgie, who had just uttered a sharp exclamation.

"Your middle finger," Georgie gasped. "Just now —when you lifted your hand——"

"Do you mean my black nail?" Patience held it up for inspection. "My brother's horse stepped on it a month ago——"

"*I* noticed that nail too," Tough said, touching Georgie's arm. "I saw it yesterday, and I thought it was a bit odd that we hadn't noticed it before. . . ."

"Patience hadn't got it before," whispered Susan, as white as a good, old-fashioned ghost. "And it takes weeks for a nail to go like that——"

"I can't imagine what all this is about," said Mrs. Kane, "but let's go into the house, anyway." She held out her hand to Patience, who backed away and then took it. "Come along, my dear. We'll straighten things out between us," she promised.

Georgie led the way, walking as if she were in a dream. On the sitting-room floor lay the crumpled copy of the Herald, and she picked it up mechanically. Once more that headline stared up at her.

> *MEDLICOTT GYMKHANA: SENSATION*
>
> The gravest anxiety is felt by all those who are acquainted with the Daneforth family, and widespread sympathy is extended to Mr. and Mrs. Daneforth, whose daughter Patience disappeared during

the Gymkhana and Horse Show held in Bartle's Meadow to-day (Friday). After distinguishing herself in several events with her usual skill, thirteen-year-old Patience was seen in the company of some unknown boys and girls, whom the police are endeavouring to trace——

The paper fell from Georgie's fingers. She must have said something, for she saw that everyone was gazing at her.

"I—think——" she began, and then went up to the girl in riding kit, who was still clinging to Mrs. Kane's hand. "You're Patience Daneforth," said Georgie. "Not Patience Best?"

At the last two words, an extraordinary change came over the other's face.

"Patience Best," she echoed. "How did you know about that?"

"Don't say," Rough began, "that Georgie's bats as well——" But a gesture from Peter silenced him, and without another word Georgie ran out of the room and up the stairs.

She went straight to the drawer where she had hidden Patience's clothes. Yes. They were still there. Then it was as she had guessed. There were—there must be —*two* Patiences. . . .

"Georgie, is that you?" called a familiar voice from the playroom, and Georgie went in at once. Patience —the real Patience, her friend from Lennet Magna— was sitting up in bed.

"I thought I heard you," she said. "I can't find any clothes, Georgie. Do get me a coat or something—I can't stay here all day. Georgie—are you angry with me? You're all so queer. I couldn't *help* being caught by the gipsies, could I?"

"Oh, Patience, we're not angry—just frightfully

puzzled. I—don't know what really did happen," confessed Georgie. "*When* did they catch you?"

"Why, after I'd stabled Timbo at the Red Dragon. I didn't have to pay—the man said, 'That's all right', as if he knew me; and another person said 'Aren't you going to ride to-day?' and offered to lend me a pony, and put me in for the last-minute entrants' race. I was feeling dazed about that when I ran into Tough, who lent me some money to buy a charm. I went to get it, and—I was seized and popped into that awful caravan. But what did *you* do when I didn't come back?" asked Patience curiously.

"You—you've got a double," Georgie muttered. "I'll tell you in a minute. She—well, she's here, as a matter of fact. Do stay where you are a bit longer while I go and speak to her."

Patience sighed and lay down, finding the situation too much for her.

As luck would have it, Mrs. Duncan had just returned to Wychwood, and now brought some breakfast up to the poor prisoner, whose head was in a whirl. Georgie ran downstairs to find that her mother had taken the other Patience into the drawing-room and made her lie down.

"You can't go in," said Gerry fussily; but the door opened at that moment.

"Is that Georgie?" asked Mrs. Kane, in a low voice. "Come in, darling. You must be very quiet, but Patience wants to ask you something." She herself came out into the hall, and they knew that she wanted to ring up the doctor.

Georgie went in and sat beside the other Patience, who was so uncannily like the one she had just left. She saw that this girl's head was painful, and she moved the cushions very gently.

"Thanks," said the stranger gruffly, and her eyes

searched Georgie's face. "I *am* Patience Daneforth, although I don't think your mother believes me. But —what did you mean by 'Patience Best'? How—how *could* you say that to me?"

"Because I know someone called that," Georgie answered stoutly, and then remembered that this was a case where humouring should be done. "Do you know a Patience Best, then?" she asked.

"No. Not really. But—I had a sister. A twin. The gipsies stole her when she was only two, and I don't really remember her, I suppose, except that I've always missed somebody. But—those were the only two words she could say. She meant, I suppose, that she liked me best of all. Twins are like that," said Patience Daneforth, and blinked. "You gave me a shock, saying that, because my old nurse has said those two words so often, and cried because Prudence was taken away all those years ago."

Georgie saw it all now, and wondered how to break the news.

"Do you think you'll ever find her again?" she ventured.

"Not now. Father and Mother did everything they could. Father always felt so guilty, because he was a magistrate, you see, and he'd sentenced a gipsy boy very harshly. That's why they took Prudence—in revenge. Oh, she may be dead by now, or anything, but it's queer—I think of her such a lot, and it shook me when you said 'Patience Best'. . . ."

"Suppose she got away from the gipsies, and someone else adopted her when she was still a baby. Suppose they *called* her Patience Best, because they thought she was saying her own name. Suppose you met someone who knew her," said Georgie, her hazel eyes shining with excitement. "Suppose she were—in this house!"

"You don't mean—you *can't* mean——"

"I'm telling you who your double is," said Georgie, "and trying to explain why we brought you here, She is upstairs, in bed, but of course she doesn't know about *you*—and I'll have to tell her even more tactfully than I've told you, because she doesn't even know that she ever had a twin——"

Georgie paused in dismay, and wondered if she had been so tactful after all. Patience Daneforth had fainted.

"Good news never kills," thought Georgie, but she called for help all the same.

It was some time before Mrs. Kane could be made to understand that there were two Patiences, for Dr. Warnford came while the strange one was still unconscious. He ordered her back to bed, so she had to be carried up to Susan's room. When she was safely settled, Georgie went in to the real Patience, as she mentally called her school friend, and began to question her about her early days with her guardian.

"But I've told you, Georgie. I don't remember anything before that—except wheels, and dark faces I didn't like, and someone tall who must have been my mother. . . ."

"No sisters? No one about your own age, whom you used to play with?"

Patience threw her a startled look.

"How queer that you should say that! I've often imagined—oh, but I'm sure lots of people do. I've pretended that I had a sister, a sort of twin, to do things with. . . ."

Georgie forgot all about being tactful.

"But you *have*," she yelled, "a real twin, plaits and all, and she's here at this moment—having concussion on Susan's bed. Oh, Paish, don't look like that—Paish, if *you* faint as well, I'll never forgive you!"

"I'm not going to faint. I'm looking for my clothes. Oh, Georgie, is it real? And is my mother——?"

"I think so. Oh, she must be. Patience spoke of her. I don't know about your father. But there's somebody called Rollo, and he's got a horse—— And your name is Prudence," Georgie finished, in a gasp, and Patience leapt out of bed and they danced a Highland fling together on the rug.

"I've pretended that I had a sister."

That was a strange, unreal morning, and perhaps the strangest part of all was when Patience Daneforth begged so hard to be allowed to see her twin that Patience Best, whom nobody could call Prudence, was told that she might go in to her for ten minutes. She was terribly nervous—more shy, even, than she had been in the train on her way to Driscoe, and she implored Georgie to go with her. But Georgie refused, so Patience went alone.

And when Georgie and Susan went to fetch her when the ten minutes were up, she was looking happier than they had ever seen her, sitting on the bed beside her twin.

"Golly," said Susan, looking at Patience Daneforth, "it's a good thing you've got that lump on your head, or we'd never tell you apart. Will you come to the Grange with Paish? Oh, I forgot—I mean Prue."

"Oh, I'm still Patience," laughed her friend, "because she's always called Pat. And what do you think? Father is alive, and Rollo is our brother, and Pat says he was at the gymkhana. And she and I had ponies before we could walk, and mine was white, called Snowball, and I remember him."

"You must remember Nannie too," said Pat. "She's got one blue eye and one brown——"

Georgie and Susan looked at each other and tiptoed away.

"We left them together," Susan told Mrs. Kane, "because they're making up for lost time. I wonder if anything else exciting is going to happen these holidays?"

"It is, my dear, and very soon too," Mrs. Kane informed her. "I've just been on the telephone to Mrs. Daneforth, telling her that her Patience is here. She and her husband are coming over right away. But they don't know yet that they have two daughters—I couldn't tell her over the 'phone. Can this be their car now?" she exclaimed, as wheels could be heard crunching to a standstill in the road.

"No, it's a van," said Georgie, "and a man's getting out with a basket. There's something sticking out—an orange-and-white striped tail. . . ."

She rushed to open the door.

CHAPTER TEN

CATASTROPHE OF CATS

GRINNING, the man opened the basket a few inches, and Georgie bent down to peep inside—fully expecting to see the features of her beloved King Toby. Alas, the feline face that met her own was a strange one, belonging to a very old and battle-scarred cat, who bristled and "fuffed" at her in a most hostile manner.

"He—isn't mine," said Georgie. "Thank you for bringing him, but——"

"He's yaller," said the man, "and I come for me five bob—see?" And he produced a torn corner of the advertisement page of the local *Herald*. Mrs. Kane leaned forward and read the lines to which his grimy forefinger was pointing:

> Five shillings reward! Anyone bringing yellow cat (golden eyes) bushy tail) to Wychwood, Dockleford, will be rewarded as above.

"Georgie, she said, in dismay, "is this what you put in?"

"Yes, Mother. Rough wanted to put, 'answering to the name of Toby', but I said no, because he doesn't always answer——"

"Darling, I don't mean that. You've put it so badly that I'm afraid you'll have to pay five shillings for every yellow cat who's brought here, whether it's Toby or not."

"Too right," smirked the man. "You don't want this ole moggy, then?"

"Where did you find him?" asked Mrs. Kane, as Georgie ran to rifle her money-box. The man shrugged.

"Wandering about Driscoe," was all he would say.

"We'll have to keep it, for the time being," said Mrs. Kane, who saw eye to eye with Georgie in matters such as these. And so the cat was taken out of its basket, given a meal, named Boxer, and sent off to make friends with Stripo.

"As if we hadn't enough to bear," remarked Gerry, "we have to open a cats' home as well. How *could* you put in such an idiotic advertisement, Georgie?"

But before anyone could answer, a big car stopped at the gate, and they all braced themselves to meet the Daneforths.

Georgie, who with Susan, Gerry, and her brothers, had decided to keep in the background, saw that the first person to get out of the car was the tall, tweedy woman they had seen in Medlicott the day before, with "Judge" pinned to her coat. She remembered seeing her speak to Patience, whom she had evidently mistaken for her twin.

After her came a frail-looking man, and then the handsome dark-haired youth who had ridden the black horse at the gymkhana. Patience's father and brother.

Mrs. Kane, after a brief conversation, took the three upstairs to the bedroom where Pat and Patience were sitting, completely absorbed in one another as they tried to piece together the lost years.

"It's the most astonishing tale I ever heard," Mrs. Kane observed, much later in the day. Her own family, who had been for a picnic with the dogs, had now returned to find that the Daneforths had gone home. "I suppose you realize that it's all through your kindness to that gipsy child that it's ended so happily?"

"Goatalina?" Susan gasped. "I don't see how she comes into it. She hated the sight of us."

"Tell us everything, Mother," begged Georgie. "Oh, who's this coming now? Another cat?"

"Two ginger kittens were brought while you were

out. I had to pay ten shillings," Mrs. Kane said resignedly. "They're so sweet, I couldn't send them away. . . . They're in the garage, with Stripo and Boxer, and there they'll stay till we decide what to do with them."

"This looks like the carrier," said Peter. "Yes, it is —it's a huge hamper addressed to Georgie in Uncle Archie's writing——"

"Oh, my hat," breathed Gerry. "I'd forgotten. I—I rang him up the evening after Toby disappeared, and asked him to find out about the Siamese kittens they have at that house next to the Great-Grandies. I wanted to give Georgie one for a surprise. I didn't know we'd be likely to collect all the cats in the west of England——"

"Gerry, how—how *good* of you," said Georgie, in amazement. "But——"

Her voice was drowned in a chorus of angry yells which proceeded from the hamper. She watched Peter open it, and gasped as a mother cat and six kittens, all sporting the Siamese (cat) colours of beige and chocolate brown, with blue eyes, leapt lightly on to the carpet and cast disdainful glances at the furniture.

"Here's a note from Uncle Archie," said Gerry, and opened it. "He says—'What a good thing you wanted a Siamese puss for Curlylocks. The owners are going abroad, and don't know what to do with Pagoda and her kittens. So you can have them all. I didn't mention it to your Aunt Marcia as I wanted to give Curlylocks a lovely, a really lovely surprise. . . ."

"Put them in the tool-shed, Rough. Not the garage, in case they fight with the others. Give them something to eat first," said Mrs. Kane. "So that was why you 'phoned Uncle Archie, Gerry."

"Yes, and it's turned out wrong—as usual," said her niece, and stalked away. But Georgie went after her.

A mother cat and six kittens . . .

"It hasn't gone wrong, and although I shall always miss Toby, it's wonderful to think that we've got eleven cats of our own. Besides, Gerry, it was so decent of you," she said, in some embarrassment. "I didn't think you minded about Toby."

"Oh, he wasn't bad," said Gerry, "and I didn't like to see you going about the place with that all-is-lost expression. But what are we going to do with them all? Open a pet shop?"

"We'll have to keep them over the week-end, anyway. Let's go back and ask Mother what she meant about Goatalina," said Georgie.

"Which Patience shall I tell you about first?" asked Mrs. Kane. "Your own, or Patience Daneforth—hereafter known as Pat?"

"Ours, please," said Susan firmly, "and oughtn't you to ring up the fishmonger and order a—a whale or something for those cats? I don't like to think of animals being hungry. . . ."

"If that means that you want supper," said Gerry, "you'll have to wait." But for once she smiled as she spoke, and Susan smiled back, rather reluctantly. After the events of the last few hours it was impossible to keep up hostilities which had, after all, very slight foundations.

"You'll *all* have to wait," Mrs. Kane said composedly, "because the haddock we were going to have has had to be used elsewhere. I've ordered the whale, Susan, or its equivalent. Now, about Patience. She was on her way to stable Timbo when she met Tough and borrowed half-a-crown, because she wanted to buy a gipsy charm. She went to the caravan, and the gipsies —who were on the look-out for Pat—naturally thought that this was the girl they wanted. They pulled her into the caravan, threw a blanket over her head, and drove off. Poor Patience—imagine how terrified she must have felt! She told me that they weren't unkind to her, though one gipsy with a squint——"

"I saw her, Mother. She's the one I bought Stripo from," put in Georgie.

"Yes. Well, she kept on reproaching Patience with something her father was supposed to have done. Of course, she was referring to a time, about twelve years ago now, when Mr. Daneforth sent her son to prison. Patience said that towards evening they came to an encampment on the moor, where her clothes were taken from her, and she had her feet tied together. They gave her food, and she saw a very old woman, who seemed like a queen, and a pretty little girl whom everybody seemed to adore. Then she realized that the little girl had gone, and that the gipsies were hunting for her. A mist came up——"

"I'll say it did," murmured Rough.

"——and after a long time one of the men said something about smelling a fire. He and another went off, and came back with little Meena, as the girl is called, and Patience says she cried out when she saw that she was wearing that scarf I've just made for Georgie—in the Grange green, and marked 'G. Kane' for all the world to see. Then there was the woolly with Susan's name-tape sewn on it, and Gerry's cardigan. So she said, "Those clothes belong to my friends', and the old gipsy asked her some questions, and, when Patience mentioned Driscoe, described Georgie in detail——"

"Then I know who she is," said Georgie, and told them about that queer conversation on the station platform. "Oh, Mother, the police won't catch them, will they?"

"I sincerely hope so," said Mrs. Kane. "However grateful the gipsies may be, they can't go about kidnapping people, can they? Look what misery they caused when they stole Patience. I wonder how her guardian came to find her, and what his reaction will be? Of course the police are looking for them, Georgie. The Daneforths informed them as soon as Pat vanished, because they had always been afraid of something like this."

Georgie nodded, remembering the story that Pat had told her.

"I still can't think how we muddled up those two at the gymkhana," said Tough.

"If we'd kept our programme, we'd have seen the name 'Patience Daneforth', and maybe we'd have guessed something," said Rough, "though it isn't likely. Other people were fooled beside ourselves. That lady—who's turned out to be Mrs. Daneforth—must have thought our Patience was her Pat when she spoke to her in the village."

"When she said something about liking her hair doubled up? Patience told me that," smiled Mrs. Kane. "And those young people who spoke to her before thought she was Pat, and that was why they were rude about poor Timbo. The Daneforths are very well off, you see; they have lots of horses and animals of all sorts and sizes."

"But Pat did loop up her hair, like Patience," said Gerry.

"Yes, she told me that when she went into the ring, with her ordinary plaits, her friends asked her why she didn't keep them doubled. She didn't know what they meant, but let someone fix them up for her. And she says she *couldn't* think who you all were, or why you took such an interest in her. Then she hurt her head and didn't want people to know—I think she's a very proud little person—and you offered to take her home. She was so dazed that she thought you meant her own home, and when she found herself being brought here, she thought her worst nightmare had come true, and that she was being abducted just as her poor little sister had been. And now what about some supper?"

Mrs. Kane glanced at Susan as she spoke, expecting to see her face light up as it usually did at the thought of sustenance. But Susan's mind was on other things.

"If we could only do the gipsies another good turn," she said thoughtfully, "they might tell us something about King Toby, and the Leadbetters' money——"

A loud knock at the front door interrupted her. A shabby-looking boy had come by bus from Driscoe, with a yellow cat tucked inside his coat.

"Five shillings, Georgie," said Mrs. Kane, extremely sorry for her rash daughter, but determined to teach her how to avoid such mistakes in future.

Georgie paid up gallantly, and the cat joined the vociferous company in the garage. Her money-box was very light now, and her heart was heavy when she remembered that Peter's birthday was on Wednesday. She had meant to buy him a book he particularly wanted, but now it would have to be a writing-pad, and a scratchy one at that.

Luckily, however, no one brought any more cats!

CHAPTER ELEVEN

SUE TAKES A HAND

THE next day was Sunday, and it seemed curiously unreal to awaken to the sound of church bells, and the knowledge that—apart from certain four-footed guests in garage and tool-shed—one was not in the middle of an adventure. Georgie lay and gazed at the sunshine filtering through the window, as she tried to sort out all the events of the last few days. Now that there was a chance to think, she found that she felt vaguely depressed. Was it because she was now unable to buy a nice birthday present for Peter? No, for she knew that he understood, and she could get him that book any time. Why, then— Surely it couldn't be because Patience, whom she had become to regard as her own property, had suddenly changed from a rather pathetic orphan to a member of a well-known family?

Georgie was shocked at herself. She was very quiet at breakfast, and afterwards, when the others went to get ready for church, she told her mother that she felt too wicked to go.

"I didn't know I *could* be so mean. But I'm afraid I'm sorry that Patience has got Pat, and a family of her own. I'd rather have her as she used to be—shy, you know, Mother, and thinking it so marvellous to be asked here to stay. . . . Oh, I'm dreadful," groaned Georgie.

"Not dreadful at all, my dear; merely honest with yourself. You're learning a hard lesson, that's all—that of seeing that someone you're fond of and want to help can get on perfectly well without you. It's a lesson we all have to learn," her mother told her. "I've had it four times already—with Peter, and the Lads, and you."

"I see what you mean," said Georgie, "though I should have thought you could have made the same lesson do for Rough and Tough, as they grew up at the same time. But I did like Patience, Mother. I mean, I do. And I don't think I shall ever like Pat."

"Oh, you will in time," said Mrs. Kane, and Patience isn't your only friend, after all. What about Susan?"

"Sue's got crowds of friends at school," grumbled Georgie, and then caught her mother's eye and laughed. "Well, I told you I was horrible," she said.

"But I'm sure that now Patience has got a twin sister and parents, you wouldn't take them away from her, so stop wallowing in remorse, and get ready for church," said Mrs. Kane. "I'm going to ask the vicar if he'd like to come and meet N'wambo."

"Oh, of course, Daddy's bringing him next week. I wonder if he'll choose Peter's birthday," mused Georgie, as she rushed upstairs to search for her hat and gloves. Gerry, immaculate from head to foot, stood and watched her frenzied hunt.

"At St. Monica's——" she began.

"Bother St. Monica's," said Georgie, pouncing on her hat, which she had used earlier in the week to hold her collection of birds' eggs while she tidied her cupboard. "I'm sick of hearing how good and tidy all the Monica-ites are——"

"I was going to say," Gerry interrupted loftily, "that one of the girls in my form who'd always thought she was an orphan found her long-lost family, something as Patience has. Only it wasn't an exciting story like this. Wonder what it feels like to be Patience?"

She spoke enviously, and Georgie glanced at her as she ran a comb through her tangle of curls.

"You talk as if *you're* an orphan, Gerry."

"Well, I'm as good as one. Father and Mother could come home from Singapore if they really wanted to see me. Oh, I'm not grousing. Auntie's very kind, and you're all decent to me. But it's like being an orphan all the same."

"Gerry!" Georgie could think of nothing more to say.

"Do buck up," said her cousin, with some asperity. "You'll make us all late."

The bells had changed from their friendly octave, which Georgie always fancied called out: *"Do hur-ry up and come to church,"* to the more urgent single note—— *"Come—come—come."* She crammed on her long-suffering hat and raced downstairs.

The vicar, who was very old, told Mrs. Kane that he would be most interested to meet N'wambo when he came, and then turned his mild, short-sighted gaze upon Georgie.

"Rumour has reached me that you have lost your pet cat," he said gently. "I never saw him, but I heard about him from various people. My wife was wondering if you would care to accept an unfortunate stray we ourselves have acquired?"

Mrs. Kane hastily explained that Georgie had a surfeit of cats already, and they all walked home, discussing the all-absorbing subject of gipsies and their ways.

Lunch was ready when they reached the house, and just as Mrs. Duncan was bringing in the roast beef, the telephone rang. Peter answered it, and announced that Mrs. Daneforth wanted to speak to Mrs. Kane. The family hovered close at hand, eager to hear news of Patience; but very little could be gathered from Mrs. Kane's brief replies. At last she replaced the receiver, and looked at her audience.

"Darlings, another time *please* don't breathe down my neck like that—you don't know how nervous it makes me. The Daneforths want you all to spend tomorrow with them, and they're sending the car over for you about ten o'clock. Won't that be fun? But a most extraordinary thing has happened. Mrs. Daneforth went over to Lennet Magna yesterday evening to interview Patience's guardian—and found that he had just died. She saw the lawyer, and has read a paper he left, to say that he found the child wandering near a gipsies' encampment, and—having recently lost his daughter and her little girl in an epidemic—yielded to an impulse and took Patience with him. This happened in Derbyshire, where the Daneforths were living at the time of the disappearance. He was moving in any case, so felt fairly safe. But he named her 'Patience Best'—believing it was her own name, or very like it—so that he would look less guilty if she were ever traced. Poor old man! He must have been very fond of her——"

"And she was very loyal to him," said Georgie, "though it must have been hard sometimes."

"Now she won't have to ride side-saddle any more," said Susan, the realist.

Talking it over among themselves, they all agreed that they didn't much want to visit the Daneforths. In a way, they all felt as Georgie did, that Patience was somehow different now that she was no longer on her own, and the Lads had reason to steer clear of Pat, who had shown them such dislike.

"*I'm* not going, anyway," said Gerry. "I shall stay at home with Auntie."

"So shall I," said Susan. "I could knock up a few meringues."

"You ought to come," Georgie pointed out, "as you're one of Paish's friends. Gerry needn't, as she isn't."

"Thanks!" Gerry snorted indignantly, and stumped away into another room to write her weekly duty letter to the parents whom she had not seen for so many years.

"Well, I thought I was pleasing her," argued Georgie, when taken to task by her mother. "She said she didn't want to go."

"Yes, but you as good as told her that she wasn't wanted. I should ask her to go if I were you. And I'll persuade Susan to defer the meringues till Peter's birthday," smiled Mrs. Kane.

Gerry took a great deal of coaxing, but at last she agreed to come. Susan was appeased by the promise of a vast quantity of sugar and eggs to play with, on the forthcoming birthday. Ten o'clock next morning found them all ready to be fetched by the Daneforths, as arranged.

"Peter, the Lads, Susan, Gerry, and myself," mused Georgie. "They'll never squeeze all of us into the car——"

"It's a big car," Mrs. Kane said inexorably, as she cooked a large amount of fish for the furry visitors, now purring and weaving round everybody's legs.

When the car arrived, however, Patience and Pat were sitting beside their mother, and it was obvious that there would not be room for six more passengers.

"I thought I'd make two journeys," said Mrs. Daneforth, standing tall and straight, with a daughter on each side of her. "If I could take four children now, and then come back for you and the other two?" she questioned, looking at Mrs. Kane.

"I didn't understand that I was included. It's very kind of you, but I'm afraid I'm not in visiting trim," laughed Mrs. Kane, and explained about all the extra work made by a dozen cats. Georgie knew that she was delighted to have this excuse, but Susan didn't think of that.

"Mrs. Duncan will look after the cats," she said, "and we'll all help with the other things when we get back."

"Yes, do come, Mrs. Kane," begged Patience, colouring in the sensitive way they remembered. She looked just the same. It was the other twin who had changed. Gone were her two plaits, for one thing, and her hair now hung straight to her shoulders, while her blue eyes looked out from under a fringe.

"I did it myself yesterday, with nail scissors," she declared, seeing Georgie's and Susan's interested gaze. "It was Nannie's fault—she said that Patience and I were like two peas in a pod. Well, it's gorgeous to have Patience, but I don't want to be in a pod with anyone

—and neither does she. So we drew lots which should look different, starting with the hair. I'll look even better when I've had time to go to a hairdresser."

"I hope so," muttered Rough.

"There's no need for you to make a second journey," Mrs. Kane told Mrs. Daneforth, once she realized that there was no chance of avoiding this visit. "I'll get our car out, and bring two or three of them in that."

While the two mothers were talking, the younger fry found plenty to say as well. Pat talked about her brother Rollo, who was waiting at home, and who, it turned out, had been to the Kane boys' school—St. John's—when he was much younger. This interesting fact broke down even Rough's hostility, though he always preferred gentle Patience to her more robust twin. Patience herself seemed so glad to see Georgie and Susan again that at first they wondered if she were not happy with her relations, and then they saw that everything was so strange to her at present that she clung to them as belonging to a more stable world. The two mothers must have seen this too, for when Mrs. Kane was ready to start, she asked the trio from the Grange to come with her. Pat, now on quite good terms with the boys, had taken Gerry under her wing as well; so they all got into the Daneforth car, which led the way.

"How lovely the moor looks," said Patience. "Just imagine—it was only last Friday that we all came over this way to Medlicott, though we didn't come by this road. How's Timbo?"

Georgie and Susan had been to see him the previous afternoon, and reported that he was quite well.

"I don't expect I shall ride side-saddle now that Guardie isn't here," Patience went on, unconsciously echoing Susan's words. "In a way I'm glad he *has* died—he'd have missed me, you see, and I shouldn't have been able to spend much time with him. He—meant so well. If he hadn't taken me as he did, I'd have grown up a gipsy—like Goatalina." Her pretty face dimpled into a smile. "I wish I could have thanked that old gipsy properly for letting me go. Goatalina's grannie, I mean. (I like your name for that child much better than Meena.) It was like a story—directly she understood who you were, Georgie, she gave me back my own clothes, and told a gipsy man to put me on the path for Dockleford. Oh, how tired and frightened I was—and what a shock I got when you all treated me like an escaped lunatic!"

They were talking and laughing so much that they did not notice that poor Mrs. Kane was having trouble with the car until the engine stalled completely, and they jerked to a standstill.

"Oh, dear, what a nuisance. I'll have to investigate," said Mrs. Kane, and she got out and opened the bonnet.

"New cars *shouldn't* do this sort of thing," Susan said sagely. "Did I tell you that Uncle James has a Lodestar like this? He showed me how to drive it—not in the road, of course. This is the starter——"

Mrs. Kane jumped back just in time as the car bounded forward and shot madly along the moorland road at some twenty-five miles an hour.

It was well for Susan that her two passengers were not people given to screaming. Georgie and Patience, though naturally alarmed, did not utter a sound to distract her as she tried to keep the car from running up one of the grassy banks. She had only the haziest idea of driving, and was simply terrified at what she had done, but she knew that the only way to avoid an accident was to keep her head. She felt with her foot for the brake, and pressed. The car seemed to spring in the air. She had touched the accelerator.

Now they were coming to a fork in the road, and, as they whizzed round a bend, Georgie saw the Daneforth's car a little way ahead. There was no room to pass, and a crash would be inevitable unless——

"Bear left, Sue," she said quietly, and Susan obeyed.

But now they had left the Medlicott road, and were on the merest cart track. The Lodestar bumped and trembled as she pursued her wild course, with Susan, her face grimly set, clinging desperately to the wheel. Then came disaster. The winter storms had brought down several tall trees, and one was still projecting half across the road. Susan swerved, but struck it, and the unfortunate car somersaulted and came to rest on springy young heather.

By a miracle the three girls climbed out, unhurt. The car itself was less damaged than one would have supposed, though the horn was jammed, and kept up a continuous wail till Susan gave it a hard bang. "Give me horses," she murmured. "They stop when they're told. . . . Oh, Georgie, what *will* your people say? I bet I'll be packed off to Uncle James."

But Georgie laid her finger to her lips, and they all listened to an oddly familiar sound.

"Mam! Ma-a-am. . . ."

"Not Goatalina! I can't bear it," cried Susan, but Patience ran forward.

"Meena—Meena," she called softly, and suddenly the bushes parted, and the Limber Elf stood before them, half shy, half defiant, but very, very curious to find out what that strange noise could have been.

So, apparently, was someone else. Another figure joined that graceful little one, and Georgie found herself looking at the old woman who had addressed her at Driscoe station less than a week ago.

"Golly," said Susan cheerfully, "I thought the police would have got you by now."

"*Hush*," implored Georgie and Patience, in an agony of apprehension; but old Sarah only smiled, proudly revealing her last remaining tooth.

"The p'lice don't want us Romany folk," she said, in her queer, high voice. " 'Tes only hedge-mumpers* like Cross-eye Molly and her kind as the p'lice wants to cotch. . . ." Her restless black eyes fixed on Patience. "I am Romany, love. I've no truck wi' kid-napping and the like."

"But the ones who did catch me took me to you," Patience said doubtfully, the old dame nodded, as she held out her thin brown hand to her great-grandchild.

"Aye, for the mist was risin' and Cross-eye Molly was scared. 'Twas her lad your father sent to jail," she told Patience, "and she's never forgotten it. But she's locked up now. P'lice fetched 'er yesterday. I never seed 'em, but there's ways of hearin' these things that gorgios** would never understand."

"Well," said Patience, "as you didn't help to steal me, I'm more than ever grateful to you for making them set me free."

"Your friends was good to Meena. Maybe ye'll come to see my caravan? 'Tes mighty better than Cross-eye Molly's. . . ."

"I'm sure it is," Patience said, with fervour, suppressing a shudder as she thought of the repulsive hovel on wheels in which she had been incarcerated. "But we can't come now, because we mustn't leave the car."

"We could leave it for a few minutes," cried Susan, winking violently at her friends and mouthing the words: "King Toby."

* Hedge-mumper—not a true gipsy. An inferior kind.
** Gorgios—people who are not gipsies.

"I suppose," said Georgie suddenly, "you haven't got a yellow cat?"

"I has," smiled Meena. "Mam give 'im to me. Come see?"

They abandoned the car at that, and "went see", as requested. Sarah's caravan, well guarded by handsome, swarthy men—real gipsies these, no hedge-mumpers—was indeed a palatial place, and in one of the windows sat a stately miniature tiger who was quite definitely *not* King Toby.

Georgie's lips quivered and she looked away. Her eyes were rather misty, so that she could not believe her own senses at first when she saw a large black book, like a family Bible, embossed with the words, "Leadbetter. Valley Farm, Dockleford."

She rubbed her eyes. It was true. She was conscious of something like disappointment. Romany or not, old Sarah was not above stealing after all.

"I know Farmer Leadbetter," she said abruptly, and saw Susan prick up her ears.

The old woman nodded serenely.

"Then maybe you'll carry his book back to 'un? My birdie's da—she has no mam but me—he took it one night last week when he came by Dockleford. I never knew—I was sleeping at the time. Once he found a couple of chicken at Valley Farm. Maybe he was lookin' for more when he stopped there that night, and peeped through the window. He knows as he shouldn't ought to've took this fine big book, but we all wants our birdie—our Meena—to be a lady and learn to read. . . ."

"I'd better take it back to them," said Georgie, picking it up. It was very heavy. "And when I get home, I'll find some nice books with pictures for Meena, and perhaps someone could fetch them."

Meena screamed for joy, and the old woman looked pleased.

"There's luck a-comin' your way, love," she told Georgie, who stepped back hastily, afraid that she would have her fortune told next. She had had enough of gipsies for the time being. In her agitation, she dropped the big book—which was not a Bible after all, but an enormous account book.

Out fluttered twenty one-pound notes.

One look at Sarah's face told the girls that the gipsies had been unaware that the money was concealed in the tome. Susan gave a whoop of joy, but Georgie went up to the old woman, who was looking terrified.

"It's all right. We'll tell them you didn't know," she said. "Meena's father oughtn't to have taken the book—or the chickens—but I'm sure the Leadbetters will forgive him. And now we must go."

"And the Romany blessing go with you," said Sarah, and she and the child watched them till they were out of sight.

CHAPTER TWELVE

HAPPY RETURNS

WHEN they got back to the unfortunate car, they found Mrs. Kane on the scene. She had hurried after it and had been badly frightened to find no sign of the girls. Once she found that they were all right, she grew very calm and said it was just bad luck, and that Susan wasn't to blame herself at all.

Meanwhile the Daneforth car had doubled in its tracks and come back to find them. Mrs. Daneforth towed the poor Lodestar to Medlicott, where it caused a minor sensation; but to everyone's relief, there was not much wrong with it, and the local garage promised to repair it in a week.

The day that had begun so badly improved as it went on, for the Kanes found that they liked the Daneforths much better than they had expected. The house, Whitelea, was beautiful, with acres and acres of lovely grounds, with woods and even a little river. Rollo and Pat showed the others round, for of course Patience had not been able to explore much of her home as yet. Rollo was in the Navy and seemed much older than his twenty years, but Georgie liked him very much, and was glad to see that he and Peter had much in common. Patience was rather shy of her handsome brother, but she was quite natural with her mother, and her quiet father, who was almost an invalid, and it was evident that she and the high-spirited Pat had almost forgotten that they had ever been parted.

"But, Georgie," Patience said urgently, as she took her friend to the stables to see Tommy Tucker, the black horse Rollo had ridden at the gymkhana, and Jacko, Pat's beautiful bay, and all the rest, "you must never think that because I've got a family now I'll be able to get on without you and Susan. I'm just the same Paish really—and I'll never forget that yours was the first real house I ever stayed in, and that if you *hadn't* asked me, I'd never have found my people. Guardie's instructions were that I was to be kept at the Grange, holidays and all, till I was twenty. He left money for that, and some to Albert, the coachman, and the housekeeper. And he must have taken a fancy to you that day you came to tea, because he's left you Prettyboy."

"A canary, of all things, in our cat-ridden house! You must have him, Patience."

"We'll go shares in him, then—just as you once said

I could go shares in your family. Oh, Georgie, won't it be exciting when we go back to the Grange and take Pat with us?"

"Yes," said Georgie, and found that she meant it. "Let's go and tell her about it."

The day passed all too quickly, for there was so much to see, from the new tennis court to the gay summer dresses which old Nannie (with one blue eye and one brown) was running up for her "Little Miss Prudence" who had been spirited away while in her charge all those years ago.

It was late when Mrs. Daneforth drove them home, her big car filled to capacity. Georgie sat dreaming in a corner, thinking of Patience's lovely new home. She would have been astonished if she had known what an important part Whitelea was to play in her own life.

They stopped at Valley Farm, and Susan gave the money to the bewildered Leadbetters, who overwhelmed them with thanks. In return, the farmer promised to let Connie keep Jet for the rest of his life, so everyone was happy.

Back at Wychwood, they found a note from Mrs. Duncan.

> Have fed cats and locked them up for night. Soup on stove only wants heating. Telegram on table is good news.

"How thoughtful of her to tell me that," Mrs. Kane said as she hurried off to find it. "Oh," she went on, reading the message, "I'm not so sure that it *is* good news. Daddy's coming home to-morrow evening, and bringing N'wambo and Teepoo with him. Oh dear, and there's nothing ready for them——"

"Never mind, Mrs. Kane, we're here," said Susan. "I can make——"

"How do you know that an African chief would *like* meringues?" snapped Gerry.

"I was going to say, I can make the beds," retorted Susan, "but I'll make the meringues too, if Mrs. Kane'll let me, because Wednesday will be Peter's birthday."

"Let's cut it out this year," Peter suggested, but nobody would allow that.

"Let's have our party just the same," said Georgie. "I expect N'wambo would like to see how a normal British family celebrates birthdays. . . ."

"Did you say *normal?*" Gerry asked nastily. "If N'wambo goes back to Africa believing that normal British families live in a perpetual state of uproar, as you do, and go chasing after gipsies, and finding people's long-lost relations, and keep twelve cats, his subjects will be told we're all crazy."

"But they'd want to come and see us all the same," said Rough. "There's nothing much wrong with us——"

"There will be soon, my smug Lad, if you don't go to bed," said his mother. "Off you go, everyone. We've a busy day ahead."

"Georgie," said Gerry, when the two girls were in bed, "I could go to stay with Margaret a day earlier. I wasn't going till Thursday, you know. But you'll want my bed for Teepoo."

"No, she can sleep in the playroom now Paish has gone. You'd like to see N'wambo, wouldn't you?"

"Well, yes," said Gerry grudgingly. "We're doing the Dark Continent for geography next term, so he'd be quite useful. But you don't want me."

"I do," Georgie said sincerely. "I like you when you're nice. Be nice and stay to meet them."

"Might as well," Gerry said in the same sour tone,

but she added, "I don't have to go to Margaret's at all. As a matter of fact, I'd rather be here."

Knowing her cousin as she did, Georgie took this as the tremendous compliment it was meant to be, and was too much overcome to reply.

Next day they all worked like beavers to get the house ready for the new guests. Georgie, whose resources were so much depleted by the purchase of cats, rushed to the village to buy Peter a cheap writing-pad, and there learned that the travelling circus would visit Dockleford on Thursday. She told the family, and they all agreed that it would make an agreeable entertainment for N'wambo.

"Then the circus people can't have had anything to do with stealing Patience," said Susan, "or they'd be in jail."

"Oh, they haven't—it was just that one family; Cross-eye Molly, and her brood. They *are* being detained at present," said Mrs. Kane, "but when they're released, Mr. Daneforth is going to do what he can for them, to make up for the harshness he showed the boy. The circus people are as innocent as Sarah and Co., who have promised to visit us every time they pass this way. What's the time? Gracious, they'll be here at any moment. Georgie, Teepoo does speak English, doesn't she?"

Georgie nodded, her hazel eyes dancing with amusement at seeing her mother so flustered. Then Tough, who had been keeping watch from a convenient bough of an apple tree, came rushing in.

"Action stations," he ordered. "Taxi sighted. Gosh, what *will* Dad say when he hears about the car?"

Susan made as if to swoon, and then waved excitedly as Teepoo's face appeared at the window, her white teeth flashing in a smile.

N'wambo proved to be a tall and magnificent figure,

with the friendly, generous nature which his daughter had inherited. He spoke very little English, and what he did know was mainly monosyllabic; but as Mr. Kane had picked up a good deal of his own language, this really didn't matter. He chose to wear white robes and a headcloth instead of European dress, and Wychwood had never before received such a picturesque guest, or one who seemed better pleased to be there.

Teepoo had evidently told him about Georgie, for he had a special smile for her, and said something which she rightly interpreted as thanks for her kindness to his daughter. He had brought necklaces of carved ivory for Georgie, Gerry, and Susan. There was also one for Patience, of course, and Teepoo's eyes grew round as Georgie told her what had happened. She turned to her father and broke into rapid, musical speech.

"Teepoo is saying that in England fairy tales can come true," said Mr. Kane.

"The circus is coming on Thursday," said Gerry. "He'll like that, won't he, Uncle?"

"Unfortunately N'wambo has to go back to London early on Thursday morning, to attend a conference with other chiefs. Teepoo will go with him, to act as interpreter on the journey. But she has promised to come to us for part of every holiday that she spends in England," said Mr. Kane, smiling at the ebony-skinned girl who looked, as usual, a model of neatness in her Grange uniform.

"Well, we'll have to make Peter's birthday party as exciting as possible," said Georgie. "I think we ought to honour N'wambo in some way."

After supper that night, her mother asked her to play a few traditional songs, which the others could sing. Georgie was always rather shy about playing, though she loved music, but she went to the piano without demur, and the African father and daughter were enthralled by the old-fashioned airs. Then Georgie, remembering that Teepoo had often spoken of a missionary at home, tried a well-known hymn, and a moment later the Europeans fell silent as the Africans sang. Teepoo's voice, seldom heard at the Grange where she was still a little nervous, was strong and sweet, but her father's was splendid. He loved singing too, and when he had finished, he came across the room and patted the grand piano as if it had been a dog.

"My father say, better than harmonium at mission," beamed Teepoo.

Next morning, she and N'wambo entered into the birthday festivities with zest. They had not brought presents for Peter, but as soon as they knew it was his birthday, N'wambo insisted upon his having a lucky elephant's tusk, and Teepoo went into the fields and picked him a bunch of wild flowers. She gave it him so simply that not even Gerry laughed.

She went for a ride with Susan that morning, and in the afternoon they all rambled on the moor with Velvet and Plush, and Rough practised his bird calls. After an early tea, Georgie and Gerry, with Susan and the Lads, retired to prepare for the entertainment they proposed to give. This was intended to be a very homely one, and they began with a charade. N'wambo was delighted and clapped vigorously. Then the Lads began to juggle, and Mrs. Kane spoke to Georgie in an undertone.

"We forgot to let the vicar know that N'wambo is here for this night only, and I know the vicarage 'phone is under repair. Fly round on my bike, please, darling, and ask him if he can come at such short notice."

Georgie obeyed, though she was sorry to miss the fun. The aged vicar opened the door himself.

"Why, yes, I think I can manage it," he said, "if I help my wife to remove some of the heavy stuff which has accumulated in the hall ready for our next jumble sale——"

Georgie was longing to go home, but the kind old man looked so tired that she felt impelled to offer to help.

"Well, if you will, I should be most grateful," he said, and showed her the bulky parcels which had been left by his parishioners. His wife was struggling to lift them. Georgie begged her not to.

"Please let me—I'm as strong as a mammoth," she said impetuously. "Where do you want them put?"

In an outhouse, they told her, and she picked up the first bundle.

"Mr. Stewart," she said, "what's that funny noise in the little shed by the back door?"

They had passed the shed several times, and she had been baffled by the queer panting and scuffling going on within.

"Oh, what you hear is our poor stray cat," said the vicar. "I found him some days ago plastered with mud and limping—I think he had been caught in a rabbit hole. So, as my wife and I could not see him suffer, although we don't care for cats, I brought him home, and bathed him, and kept him in that shed where we store our potatoes and onions. Tomorrow I must ask Mr. Jones of Driscoe to take him away."

They went back for the remainder of the parcels. As they passed the shed this time, they heard a loud, heartrending miaou. Georgie turned white and dropped what she was carrying—a bundle of old clothes, luckily.

"Mr. Stewart," she panted, "may I open the door?"

"If you don't let him escape——"

But the orange form that leapt out of captivity had no intention of escaping. King Toby, decidedly crestfallen but as beautiful as ever, sprang into Georgie's arms and purred like an electric drill.

"I cannot tell you how sorry I am," poor Mr. Stewart said several times, in great distress. "But I had

King Toby sprang into Georgie's arms.

never seen your cat, and when I found him that day he looked a most pitiable object."

"So the gipsies never had you at all," Georgie whispered to her pet, as he made French knots all over the new blouse she had donned in honour of N'wambo, "and we needn't have gone chasing off into the wilds. But, oh, Toby, if we hadn't, we'd never have found Patience's people, or the Leadbetters' money or gone to the gymkhana, or met the gipsies, or found out that old Gerry isn't so bad after all. . . . So you haven't suffered in vain, King Toby, though to-morrow you shall have the biggest fish we can buy, to make up for all these days in durance vile. . . ."

But that didn't sound very polite to Mr. and Mrs. Stewart, so she apologized and hurried home with Toby, leaving the bicycle to be collected later.

Susan was waiting for her, and greeted the cat as if he really were a king returning from exile.

"It just wanted this to make things perfect," she said, as she patted his head and made horse-noises to him, as she knew little of smaller animals. "You were gone such ages that we didn't know what to do to amuse N'wambo, and at last the Lads fetched in all the cats——"

"Help! I'd forgotten them," groaned Georgie.

"Wait a minute. N'wambo was thrilled to bits, because he meant to take some English cats home with him—wants to start a new strain—and he thinks they were got especially for him. So he's having them all shipped to Africa. Doesn't it just *show* how things right themselves if one leaves them alone?"

"H'm," said Georgie, not sure of her friend's philosophy, but far too happy to argue. "Things have certainly worked out all right this time. Let's hope they'll keep on doing it." She spoke with feeling, suddenly thinking of next term, when she would learn to ride, and assume new responsibilities at the Grange, where she and her friends would no longer be considered "new". The school would be far bigger than it had been in its memorable first term, and Pat Daneforth would be there. . . .

Then she shook off her momentary apprehension. This was Peter's birthday, and everyone was enjoying it, and King Toby had come back. She handed him carefully to Susan.

"Show him to the others, will you? But explain to N'wambo that *this* cat's not for export. Tell them all

I'll be with them in a minute—but everything's so wonderful," she said, "that I've simply got to ring up Patience. Oh, and, Sue, tell Mother that the vicar *is* coming to supper. By the way, how are your meringues?"

For answer, Susan gave a strangled wail and thrust King Toby back at Georgie before rushing into the kitchen. There was the sound of the oven door opening, and the smell of burnt sugar. Then Susan's voice, valiant in defeat, called gaily:

"I've made some wizard hardbake. Funny, I just said that things looked after themselves if one left them alone. Er—have you a chisel, please?"